COLIN
WHO?

THE AUTOBIOGRAPHICAL
RAMBLINGS OF THE ACTOR

COLIN SPAULL

COLIN
WHO?

THE AUTOBIOGRAPHICAL
RAMBLINGS OF THE ACTOR
COLIN SPAULL

FIRST EDITION
First published by Fantastic Books Publishing 2020
ISBN (ebook): 978-1-912053-32-2
ISBN (paperback): 978-1-912053-31-5

In loving memory of my grandson Oliver Robert Faulkner

29\06\00 – 06\10\09

Forever in my heart Ollie

Grandad loves you.

FOREWORD

BY FRAZER HINES

Dear reader, here is the foreword to my good friend Colin's book.

The book has been a long time coming, but there again he has been a long time acting! I first met Colin or "Clin Splat" as he was known (more of that later) many moons ago.

Once upon a time there were lots of little boy actors roaming the streets of London on the way to auditions. If it was a film then Richard O'Sullivan usually got it, if a TV show, then usually Colin or myself.

The TV series we first met on was *Heidi* in 1959, the producer was Joy Harrington. Colin played Peter the goatherd and I was in an episode as an organ grinder. The monkey was already cast, otherwise …? Then he was Pip in the BBC's *Great expectations* whilst I played Jan in the BBC's *The silver Sword*.

These two shows set us on the way to fame and fortune. Oh yes, fame … so much so, that years later we were at the All Stars Gala at Battersea Park and ended up being chased by screaming girls trying to rip our clothes off, which made a change from us chasing girls trying to rip their clothes off! We took refuge behind a barrier and signed so many autographs that his ended up as "Clin Splat".

Then Colin found puberty (funny name but a nice lass) and I was whisked into the universe with Doctor Who and we lost touch. I'm so glad that Doctor Who brought us back together at a convention, and from that day onwards our friendship has rekindled, and we spend many happy days on Doctor Who cruises.

I know you'll love this book and there's no point me telling you of all the famous people he's worked with because he will tell you himself. Read on …

Frazer Hines

PROLOGUE TO ACT ONE

The weather was vile, and an icy blast was running up my left trouser-leg, chilling all it found at the end of the tunnel before roaring down my right leg, sending shivers into my toes. Ahead of me stood the ladder I was expected to climb to reach my seat in the commentary box at Gillingham FC's ground in Kent.

I don't usually have a problem with ladders – occasionally, when times were hard, I worked as a builder's labourer and hod-carrier, but I was a bit younger then. A man of my age should definitely not be expected to climb ladders under any circumstances, let alone in the open air and in weather like this.

Yet, here I was about to climb the one to the next step in my film career, starring as a football commentator in *Make Aliens Dance*, a short film destined to be shown at a major film festival in the States.

Looking back over my life, I find myself at a bit of a loss to know how it all came about.

Time for some detailed reflections … Should I look backwards from today or forwards from the 1940s? I've spent most of my life before a TV camera, a film camera, a microphone, or footlights. What, though, was the last truly memorable thing I did? Was it as bad as this?

In my line of work you often find yourself being abused, sometimes verbally, sometimes physically, and occasionally both, such as when I appeared in *Catherine Tate's Christmas Show* on BBC Television. In 2015 I played Ms Tate's hapless neighbour, Bernie, who despite the indignities he suffers at her hands, including being knocked to the ground and sprayed with foam from a fire extinguisher, remains resolutely infatuated with the repulsive Nan character. I shouldn't complain; she managed to humiliate almost everyone in the show, even Warwick Davis who had done nothing to deserve it!

It was an interesting experience, but one which gave me pause for thought; how had I, a South London boy whose family weren't actors or entertainers, come to be watched by millions of people as I endured such treatment? It then occurred to me that I was probably starting at the wrong end; life is after all a story, with a beginning, a middle and … well, let's not get morbid!

CHAPTER ONE

THE VERY EARLY YEARS

It all started in May 1944 at a maternity hospital in Oriental Road, Woking, where my mother had gone into hiding from Mr Hitler's forces; perhaps my dad's efforts (as an aircraft mechanic in the Fleet Air Arm) to bring about the defeat of the Axis powers had upset Adolf and he was bent on revenge.

Before I came along my mother worked for an insurance company in central London, which must have been a very demanding job, what with blackout-related car-crashes, burglaries and the like. Her ploy evidently worked because here I am, seventy-something years on and still (touch wood) in reasonably good health.

The same cannot unfortunately be said of my late brother Peter, who would have been a couple of years or so older than me but who died in infancy. I have no memory of him and didn't learn of his existence until I was in my mid-teens. I still find myself wondering what it would have been like to have had a big brother. Would I still have gone to drama school? Been a child-star? A bit famous? Would my life have been better or worse? It would almost certainly have been different. Perhaps he would have talked me out of some of the many mistakes I've made, or perhaps he would have outshone me as an actor. We'll never know, but somehow that never stops me from speculating.

When many years later our son Elliot was born my wife Sally and I agreed to give him the middle name Peter in honour of the brother I never knew.

My first home was a council flat in a block called Elms House in Pascal Street, South Lambeth, just a bit south of the river (Thames) in London. It was on about the sixth floor, as far as I can remember, and I don't recall there having been a lift, which was bad luck on anyone needing to take heavy shopping and/or a perambulator to its front door. I suspect it was also the curse of the coal man. It had been built well before the era of central heating and double-glazing, and probably contributed much to our current problem with global warming. Maybe it should have been renamed with that in mind – 'Trump Tower' perhaps? It did however possess 'all mod cons', i.e. an indoor bathroom and loo, and in order to discourage the use of the bath for solid-fuel storage there was a designated coal cupboard, complete with removable planks. The idea was that you slotted said planks into special grooved tracks in the wall just before a new delivery of coal, then as you used the stuff and the pile went down you removed the planks to improve access to your remaining stock. If you were lucky (or as rumour had it, young, female and attractive) and if he was not too breathless from carrying two hundredweight sacks of fuel up all those stairs the coal-man would put the planks in place for you.

We didn't cook on a coal-fired stove though; we had a gas cooker. Gas in those days was very very poisonous, and so they made it very very smelly.

Like most people we had a slot meter. I think it ate sixpences and shillings (2½p and 5p coins in today's money) and every so often a man would come round and empty it. The meters were set to overcharge you by a few percentage points, so the customer was always entitled to a rebate when the meter was emptied, provided it had not been tampered with. Some people treated them as piggy-banks, making withdrawals (with the aid of a screwdriver) when times were hard then claiming to have been burgled. No rebates for them! Counting all those coins was a lengthy process, and the official would sometimes accept a cup of tea – his criteria being, I suspect, similar to those employed by the coalman in deciding whether or not to help with the planks. The rebate was often several shillings, which may not sound much these days but back then would have been enough for a housewife to have her hair done with change left over for a bottle of scent.

Just opposite our block of flats was Wilcox Road, which was host to a lively street market, now sadly no more. Back in 2011 there was a suggestion by the Vauxhall Society that the market should be revived but as far as I can tell it came to nothing, perhaps because the site would have been very close to a large supermarket.

People used to shop on a more-or-less daily basis because hardly anyone had a fridge and home freezers were almost unheard of. I'm not sure that was altogether a bad thing. It probably meant that the food we ate was fresher, and with rationing still in force and food still being comparatively expensive there was probably a lot less wastage.

We have, I suppose, come a long way since then. I can't help recalling though, whenever I hear somebody saying that such and such is 'the best thing since sliced bread', the day my mum sent me on an errand to buy something (I forget what) and I saw a huge (to me, aged very few years) crowd of people standing outside the baker's shop. They were evidently fascinated by whatever was in the window. It took a while, but I managed to get myself through the milling throng to a point where I could see what they were looking at, and it was indeed a remarkable sight.

In the window was a machine, and it was actually slicing bread. The baker was just feeding in each loaf and letting the machine cut it into wonderfully neat, even slices. In those days most people relied on the humble bread-knife, and sandwiches therefore tended to resemble doorsteps in terms of thickness because cutting thin slices was quite difficult. I still don't know how people can make Melba toast.

I must have spent ten minutes watching that machine, maybe longer, and I expect Mum was a bit worried, though less so than a mother would have been today; we may have had sliced bread but 'stranger danger' had not yet been invented.

The whole area had been severely damaged by bombs during the Second World War, so the wide open spaces I and other kids played on were mostly cleared bomb-sites. I don't suppose parents today would let their kids (aged four and upwards) play unsupervised amongst the rubble and Heaven knows what else they were liable to encounter in such places, but we just took it in our stride. At that age you don't think too much about how or why such playgrounds came into existence.

My best friend Peter Stubbs and I (we went to Primary School together and still see each other from time to time, the better part of seventy years on) preferred them to the official playgrounds with swings and what-have-you. Maybe it was because those were populated by younger kids with their mothers in attendance.

My first stage appearance at Butlins in 1950. I'm number 195

Boys in those days expected and received the freedom to get up to mischief. Today's lads by comparison are almost always under adult supervision and, apart from riding their bikes on the pavement, have to be pretty law-abiding. We weren't. I'm not saying we were mugging people or breaking into houses; what we did was definitely not serious crime, but on the other hand, Saturday morning cinema was fair game.

It cost ninepence to get into the Granada to see the likes of Roy Rogers, Hop-along Cassidy and Tarzan, who was played in the serial version by an actor called Lex Barker. My little group of mates and I used to love watching Tarzan as he rescued beautiful women from all sorts of tricky situations, wrestled with crocodiles and performed feats of archery which would have put Robin Hood to shame.

The problem was that ninepence was a lot of money in those days, especially for a primary-school kid who was lucky if he got sixpence (2½p) a week pocket money. Our solution was to club together and purchase just one ticket. The boy with that ticket would then go into the auditorium and take a seat as close to the front as he could and slightly off to one side. Once the lady with the torch, known back then as an usherette, had returned to her post at the rear entrance he would surreptitiously make his way to the fire door, open it and let the rest of us in. We would try and stay quiet and inconspicuous as we found seats for ourselves. We usually got away with it, but sometimes the manager, aware that he was losing about two shillings and threepence (11p) a week, stationed one of his usherettes by the fire door to prevent people from sneaking in for free.

We still managed to see quite a lot of films though, and were lucky enough to be inside when Lex Barker made a personal appearance on the stage of the Granada one Saturday morning. We were hugely excited to meet our hero, and once it was over we ran off down the street, all whooping and shouting in what we fondly believed to be a Tarzan-like manner.

Another activity we enjoyed was swimming. You may have seen the film *Passport to Pimlico*, where residents converted a bomb-site into a lido. Our swimming pool was nothing like that; we used the Nine Elms Public Swimming Pool and Bath House. I don't think the water in the pool was heated – it could have served as the inspiration for the Nine Elms Cold Store they later built nearby – but it was still good fun. If you're wondering about the 'and Bath House' bit, remember that it was built before the war when indoor plumbing was still rather primitive and few working-class homes had a bathroom, so such public bathing facilities were very necessary.

Using the swimming pool was not expensive, so when we came out we usually had enough money for a packet of broken biscuits, costing one old penny, and maybe even a bag of lemonade powder, which was bright yellow, fizzed on your tongue like sherbet and stained your fingers so badly that parents would (laughingly) accuse you of being on forty Capstan Full Strength cigarettes a day. Nowadays that would cost you about a hundred quid, assuming you could find any for sale. I think they've been banned under the Geneva Convention as a weapon of mass destruction.

The area where I spent those early years has changed beyond recognition. Not even the gasworks, so long a contributor to the exciting smell of the place, survives, and I see from a well-known mapping and imaging service that Elms House also appears to have been demolished. I mourn their passing, and at the same time I'm surprised that not so much as a small blue plaque has been provided to mark my stay in the area and commemorate my illustrious career. Perhaps some current resident chancing to read this tome will feel able to exert the necessary pressure to persuade the Council to rectify its mistake.

My father came home from the war a year or so after my birth. I can't remember exactly when, but I'm told that he started work almost straight away as a lift-mechanic at the Ministry of Works, the department then responsible for all Government building projects as well as the release of land and property requisitioned for war-time purposes. His job had its ups and downs, and was not all that well-paid, so to earn a few bob extra he moonlighted as a scenery-shifter at London's Garrick Theatre when productions changed. That connection with the theatre may or may not have influenced him to accept my eventual choice of profession but it did contribute to his being one of the first people in our street to own a car and a TV set. The latter made us popular on Coronation Day. I don't know how many people there were huddled around that set to watch its tiny screen, but it was a lot.

In due course we were able to move out of central London to a bungalow in a slightly less war-torn suburb called Worcester Park, which was then in Surrey but is now part of the London Borough of Sutton.

However, I'm getting ahead of myself; you've bought this book because you want to know all about me so I mustn't leave out anything of importance unless its inclusion would render me liable to legal action.

Returning to the mid 1940s, to a London very different from today's and to a Britain that had not yet invented the National Health Service, which meant that medical treatment was a luxury not everyone could afford. I was fortunate; my parents numbered amongst the few who could, so that when I was about fourteen months old and measles did strange and unpleasant things to my eyesight they were able to have me treated. I have to say that the treatment was not always pleasant or enjoyable, to put it mildly, and there were times when (had I understood such things) I might have wished my parents were poorer. However, they weren't, so when my left eye decided it wanted to have a look at its right-hand colleague and turned itself in that direction I was able to have corrective surgery.

It took the surgeon, a Miss Dollar, three goes to get it right. That probably wasn't her fault. I somehow managed to break the stitches a couple of times. Even so, all that surgery didn't cure the problem, and for several years I was a regular attender at an eye hospital. I recall it being a very gloomy austere sort of place, with a white-tiled area where you waited we hard wooden benches, the only entertainment provided being an elderly nun who would go round asking children questions and rewarding them if they answered correctly. I only remember getting one question right. I don't know how old I was, it was a very long time ago after all, but perhaps it speaks volumes about both my appreciation of the value of money and the limitations of my mathematical ability.

The question was, 'How many pennies are there in a pound?' The answer, of course, was two hundred and forty, and my reward was just one of them.

In those days, a penny (1d not 1p) was worth having. The coins were about four times the size of today's fiddly little things, and in any given handful you might find pictures of one queen and up to three different kings on the heads side. I seem to remember that there were two versions of Queen Victoria still circulating in those days: the 'bun penny', with dates between 1860 and 1894, and the later 'widow' or 'veiled' series, issued in the last seven years of her late Majesty's reign. OK, I confess. I looked that up on the internet, but I still think our old money was more interesting than today's.

Furthermore, you could actually buy things with pennies and could even travel quite a long way on a bus for just a couple of the things. People would sometimes describe a long journey as 'a fourpenny bus-ride'.

Having failed to make much of a fortune in the waiting area I would in due course find myself in the treatment zone, where scary-looking people armed with menacing machines would do inexplicable things to me. Looking back, those tests and treatments made perfect sense, but I was only a child and so merited even less by way of explanation than would a grown-up patient. Occasionally they had the sense to try and make a game of it. The operation had left me cross-eyed, and there was a strong risk of my ending up with a lazy eye; in fact, I still suffer from something similar to the extent that I cannot appreciate 3D films or television.

The treatment consisted of alternating left- and right-eye patches, and the test of how well I was doing was my ability to put a lion in a cage. Not a real lion, you will understand, just a picture of one. I now realise, as I'm sure do you, that I speak of an instrument called the Clement Clarke Synoptophore. The test subject had to look through something a bit like the eyepiece of a submarine's periscope, complete with knobs on the side. One eye would see the image of a cage, the other that of a lion. When the eyes were working together correctly the lion appeared to be inside the cage, but when it wasn't they weren't. The operator asked me where the lion was in relation to the cage then instructed me to twiddle the knobs to adjust a prism and appear to put the lion in the cage. How much twiddling I did was recorded and compared to previous tests to see if the eye patches were having the desired effect. I sometimes wonder how many of my fellow patients grew up to become animal rights activists, but at the same time I am grateful that the treatment seems to have worked, and my vision is fairly normal provided I stay away from 3D television sets and the like.

Nevertheless, it was a lengthy treatment, and was still going on when

I started attending the Priory Road Primary School in (surprise surprise) Priory Road. It was about ten minutes' walk from our flat. As both my parents were working I used to go to one of Mum's friend's after school. She was called Ethel Ashe and had a son called Roger who was in my class. We were quite good friends so it all worked out well.

For some reason I changed schools after a couple of years; I don't think I was expelled from Priory Road. I don't remember doing anything quite bad enough to warrant that. But I completed my primary education at Springfield Primary School in Crimsworth Road.

That school seems now to have sunk without trace. I can't tell you much about it. It wasn't the most memorable of schools and seems now to have been closed for a very long time. I was there for three or four years, so it's possible, though not very likely, that someone out there will recall my earliest attempt to become an actor, when I was cast in my first speaking (or rather 'squealing') part in a class production of *The Three Little Pigs*.

My mother obviously thought I had talent and encouraged me in my efforts, even going so far as to take me to Ellisdon's joke shop in Holborn, where she bought me a suitable mask. I also wanted their black-face soap and one of those nail-through-the finger tricks and some stink-bombs and … and … and … but as she often told me, 'I want doesn't always get.' I've since learnt it was a popular saying amongst parents in that era of post-war austerity.

As to the play, if anyone remembers witnessing what I am sure was a truly landmark performance could they please remind me which building material I selected? I suspect that decision may have affected the way my life turned out.

Equally forgotten nowadays is the secondary school I attended in

Tennyson Road, Battersea. No trace of it remains now, but I owe a huge debt of gratitude to one of its teachers, a Mr Probert. He it was who suggested to my parents that I should take acting lessons at the Italia Conti School, then based in Archer Street in the heart of what they now call Theatre Land. It has since moved several times, even spending a year or two south of the river in Lambeth before ending up in its present home near London Wall in the Barbican.

I think it might have been the ease with which I seemed able to learn and recite poems that persuaded Mr Probert it would be a good idea; I have been lucky in having that sort of memory because the ability to learn lines is extremely useful in the acting profession. Unfortunately it's an ability that seems to diminish in later life. I'm not sure I could cope with too many long speeches these days.

Perhaps because of his connection with the Garrick my father accepted the suggestion and in due course I was auditioned by Miss Ruth Conti, who was the niece of the school's founder and who taught there for many years. She had managed to see it through the Second World War, keeping it open despite the destruction of its original home in Lambs Conduit Street. She lived to be 101, dying in Sydney, Australia, in November 2015.

Italia Conti started out as an actress, but was asked by theatrical producer Sir Charles Hawtrey (not the one in the *Carry On* films) to teach the younger members of the cast of a children's play, *Where the Rainbow Ends*, by Clifford Mills and John Ramsay, with incidental music by Roger Quilter. Sorry, I'm getting off the point a bit here. Just think of it as my attempt to give you slightly better value for money. You never know, it might come up in pub quiz and you'll thank me for telling you.

She evidently enjoyed her task and performed it well, for she went on to found the school which still bears her name and which is probably the oldest of its kind in Britain, and indeed, the world, having its origins several years before the First World War. Famous former pupils include Sir Noël Coward, Clive Dunn (L/Cpl Jones in *Dad's Army*), Wendy Richard (*Are You Being Served* and *EastEnders*), William Hartnell (the first ever Doctor Who), Leslie Phillips (voice of the Sorting Hat in the *Harry Potter* films, veteran star of Radio, TV and theatre), Zaraah Abrahams (*Coronation Street, Waterloo Road*) Anthony Newly, Jack Hawkins, the list is huge. I live in hope that one day they'll get round to putting me on it. If you want to see more just type 'Italia Conti alumni' into your search-engine.

Back to the story; I can't remember what I performed by way of an audition. I think it was either Hamlet's soliloquy, that bit in *Henry V* about imitating the actions of the tiger or the full version of *Eskimo Nell*, but it doesn't really matter as they accepted me anyway, first as a Saturday student then a year or so later as a full-time pupil.

It was plain they had much to teach me, starting with how to speak Posh.

'No dear, your birthday's in MEY, not MY.'

The problem was that my accent showed very clearly that I was a South London boy. Back then, and we're taking about the 1950s, don't forget, people expected actors to use something called Received Pronunciation, defined as 'the standard accent of English as spoken in the south of England.' Note that it says England, not London.

If you were going to perform the works of Shakespeare, so the theory went, you had to speak with the accent he would have used. How can that have been anything other than the way Winston

Churchill and the Queen spoke? It was, of course. He was born in the Midlands and probably had a Warwickshire accent, but as that county is neither Oxfordshire nor Cambridgeshire and a long way from London we ignored that.

So, much recitation of phrases such as 'The rain in Spain' and 'How now brown cow' and other exercises worthy of Henry Higgins himself was the order of the day ... or week ... or (and so it felt) year. *My Fair Lady* was on the verge of being a big hit at the time.

Tedious, but looking back, probably a good investment of my time, for it not only instructed me in the art of speaking 'properly', it also taught me how to adapt my voice to other accents, a skill which was later to allow me to take on roles using all manner of different accents except, of course, Geordie. You can only speak that properly if you're born within the smell of the Tyne. (Sorry, north easterners!)

CHAPTER TWO

AN ATTEMPTED EDUCATION

As I was about to tell you a few pages back, we eventually moved away from our council flat in South Lambeth to more spacious accommodation in Worcester Park, which in the early 1950s was still almost a country area.

My parents had been looking to move for some time; Dad was doing well at work, and they were able to afford to take on a mortgage. Looking through local papers, they eventually came across the bungalow in which they were destined to spend most of their married lives. They bought it for around £2000, though it's worth a bit more now.

I can just about remember the excitement of moving. Our new home was one of quite a number that had been built along what was then an unadopted road. You don't see many of those nowadays, but back then they were quite common. Ours had started life as a private road on land owned by someone who had, I suspect, fallen on hard times and had had to sell off some of his estate to property developers.

The word 'unadopted' here means that the local council didn't have to look after it, so that despite being occasionally re-surfaced with fresh gravel it soon developed enough puddles and potholes to render it challenging for the suspension of all but the most robust of motor cars.

The road was eventually adopted by the council and its surface improved. There was pristine tarmac, and the pavements had brand-new flag-stones. All very smart. Until a few weeks later when the Post Office decided to lay telephone cables under the street, and dug a lot of it up again. Nothing changes.

I must have been about twelve or thirteen when we moved, and had probably started at drama school, which I greatly preferred to the Secondary Modern school I started out in, but talk about culture shock! Until I started at Conti's I'd barely heard of William Shakespeare but that was all about to change.

The thought of becoming a Shakespearian actor had never entered my head. I think I saw myself as more likely to become a circus clown, wearing big shoes and a red nose in the hope of making people laugh. Before long though I found myself in Foyles in the Charing Cross Road buying copies of *Richard III*, *Titus Andronicus* and other plays about assorted Henrys, some apparently with built-in commercial breaks. I cannot claim to have liked or even properly understood the works – the term 'gobbledegook' comes to mind – but my efforts were eventually to be rewarded when I found myself appearing at London's Old Vic Theatre playing the juvenile leads in those self-same plays.

This was back in 1957. I was only just into my teens and had not been a Conti-boy for very long. I have to say though that despite all that, and even before the bruises had faded (of which more anon), I felt tremendously honoured actually to have been a part of that season. It was after all one of the best and most prestigious theatre companies in the country, perhaps even in the whole world.

I had been asked to audition. Conti's, the agency side of the school was representing me at that time, had put me up for the job and I duly went along to the theatre in Waterloo Road, not far from the station, accompanied by my chaperone as required by law.

I was ushered on to the stage from the prompt side, stage left; no bastard prompt (see chapter 5) at the Old Vic, and the first thing I saw was an almost completely empty auditorium, with just a few people near the front. I don't know why, but empty seats can be almost as intimidating as ones sat on by critics. I remember being somewhere between a bit nervous and absolutely petrified; closer to the latter, if I'm honest.

They didn't introduce themselves but I guessed that one of them was the director. Somebody handed me a piece of paper. On it was a speech from the play being cast, Shakespeare's *Richard III*, which I was asked to read.

Fortunately I was quite good at sight-reading. The trick is to allow your brain to go first. With practice you can subconsciously read a line or two ahead so that the bit of your brain that's working on the words your eyes are focusing on has some idea of what's coming next and can instruct your voice accordingly. At least, that's what I read somewhere (though not aloud).

Anyway, however I did it I must have got the phrasing and intonation about right and to have managed to stop too much South London from creeping into my delivery because I got the part and stayed there for the rest of the Shakespeare season, taking the juvenile leads in *Henry VI Part 3* and *Titus Andronicus,* as well as *Richard III.*

However, I am (as usual) getting ahead of myself. Before I could work in such an august company I had teeth in need of cutting.

My first paid work was of a very sedentary nature, just sitting or lying down in front of a camera. Yes, I was a model before I was an actor. Supermodels had yet to be invented and I didn't become famous. In fact, when my picture was used in an advertisement for dog food the pooch got more space than I did. That phase of my career was followed by brief 'walk-ons' as a child extra in various films, doing undemanding things like playing in the street behind the grown-ups who were doing serious stuff. I must have been quite good at it, though, as it wasn't long before I was allowed to go on to real stages in real theatres. That meant that I was effectively earning my keep. Conti's combined the roles of school and theatrical agency and would apply my earnings partially to offset my school-fees.

Following that Shakespeare season at the Old Vic my next stage appearance was at the Theatre Royal, Windsor, in a play called *The Remarkable Mr Pennypacker*. Also in the cast was a very young Prunella Scales, with whom I was to work again in *The Secret Garden* in 1960. Much to my relief and slightly to my surprise we all came through it unscathed. Nobody booed, no rotten fruit was thrown. It all went really well. That was encouraging, but didn't cure my first night nerves; it just helped me to cope with them.

Although that engagement only lasted a couple of weeks it was soon followed by others and I found myself travelling around the country, even as far afield as Northampton, where I played a boy called Hopcroft Minor in John Dighton's play *The Happiest Days of Your Life.*

Some thirty years later I toured in that same play with Richard Murdoch and the well-known comedian Charlie Drake – but not in the same part! It was not a very successful tour, and ended in our wondering if we would see a single penny of the promised fee. Charlie

"Hello my darlings" Drake was perhaps no longer the box-office draw he had once been, and Dicky Murdoch's retention of lines was not as good as it used to be. My enduring memory is of having accepted a lift from Dicky in his rather large and extremely luxurious BMW. He had, I was to discover, a nasty habit of spreading a map across the steering wheel and peering at it intently as he drove, with only occasional glances at the road. I was grateful when he accepted my offer to give him a break from driving and allowed me to drive. However, yet again, I digress …

My commitment to working in theatre meant that I spent rather less time in school than most boys of my age. Absence from school wasn't treated quite as seriously as it is today, when parents can be fined for taking their kids on holiday during term-time, but there was still a bureaucratic process to go through, as well as a medical examination, for which I had to go to County Hall on the South Bank. The building is now an hotel, but in those days it was the main office for London County Council.

I remember the medical examination as quite thorough. As well as the usual checks of heart, lungs and reflexes, there was the dreaded 'Can you cough for me, please?' Apparently I was sound in wind and limb so I was able to get the requisite LCC licence.

From then on I received some fairly basic lessons from a tutor back-stage when I was working. When I was resting (actor-speak for unemployed) I was allowed to sit at the back of a classroom at Conti's learning not English or Geography but the lines for my next job. Despite the best efforts of Italia Conti's teachers and roving tutors my education seems to have suffered. I can't say I mind though; the joy of having worked with wonderful people like Prunella more than makes up for not knowing the population of Winnipeg or understanding Heisenberg's uncertainty principle.

Those who say I'm badly educated may be right but I'm not really sure. I did get a good grounding in drama, singing and dancing (ballet, tap and ballroom: note to the producers of *Strictly*: I'm available!) – the minimum skill-set for anyone seriously intent on a career in theatre.

Outside school hours I enjoyed a considerable amount of freedom. More so, in some ways, than I did when I was working, when until the day I turned fifteen I always had a chaperone looking after my moral welfare backstage.

When we weren't working my friends Graeme Harper, Hugh Janes and I learnt quite a few things not found in the normal school curriculum by exploring the area around the school. It was right opposite the stage door of the Windmill Theatre, which was still in those days a very naughty place where naked ladies abounded, mostly, to our intense regret, behind doors which remained obstinately closed to lads of our age. The ladies appearing at the Windmill were not allowed to move on stage, the Lord Chamberlain having famously decreed, 'If it moves, it's rude.'

Even so they were something I really wanted to see, and I considered using my new-found skill in applying make-up to age myself sufficiently to get past the doorman, but never put the plan into execution. I think it was my lack of a suitably dirty Mackintosh that prevented me from trying; it was obviously some sort of uniform and was worn by most of the men who went in and out of the place.

I did get to know a few of the women who worked the streets of Soho. They were on the whole a friendly bunch, though they would tease me that I was far too young for them and tell me to come back when I was older and had lots of money saved up. That was likely to take some time. Even though I was getting quite well-paid as a child-actor, I saw very little of what I was paid.

My school, also my agent, took a cut of my wages; the balance was sent to my parents, who didn't have bank accounts and thus relied on the services of a lady in the Wandsworth Road to cash the cheques. I just received pocket money, which always seemed to be a bit less than I needed. My friends were in much the same boat, so even when we were feeling flush we used to use the cheaper and more cheerful (though possibly less hygienic) restaurants such as The Dairy in Great Windmill Street or the Wimpy Bar in Shaftsbury Avenue. On special occasions we went to the slightly more up-market Lyons Corner House in Piccadilly, where we were served by attractive young ladies known as Nippies. However, we were never big tippers so I'm not sure we were very popular there.

Once I became better known as a child actor and also a bit richer I developed more expensive tastes. There was a particularly good Chinese restaurant on Shaftesbury Avenue, not far from the Wimpy Bar in terms of distance but way ahead of it in terms of exciting food. By today's standards it wasn't very expensive. 4/6d (22.5p) would buy a teenager a pretty decent set meal. I remember once they gave me a present, an ornate Chinese fan in a metal container. I can't recall ever getting anything else from them, and as I was by then a reasonably well-known television actor and already had a few fans I gave it to my mother. I think she liked it, but I don't remember ever seeing her use it.

Roaming the streets of Soho was fun in those days; there was an all-pervasive air of naughtiness about the place which has largely gone now. I was young when I started exploring the area so some of what went on was mystifying. I remember seeing lots of doors with cards saying 'Model upstairs'. For some reason I thought they must be selling Airfix kits, on which I was quite keen at the time, but I wasn't sure and I never climbed those stairs. Honest!

Being in the heart of Theatreland meant that it was easy for us to see many of the shows in the area, at theatres where I was later to appear. *Oliver, My Fair Lady* and *Hair* come to mind (especially the latter, though I would deny that that was just because it featured full-frontal nudity). I think that given the choice and despite TV and film work being both fun and in some ways, especially financially, more rewarding, I would rather have worked exclusively in theatre, preferably in the West End. I think I've played most of London's theatres, of which there are a lot, though sadly fewer than there used to be. I have fond memories of the old Stoll Theatre on Kingsway, on a site now occupied by part of King's College. I could mention more – Wyndham's, the Vaudeville, the Victoria Palace, and the Aldwych, for example – but I won't bore you with a full list. Suffice it to say that I've trodden the boards in most of them.

Soho was then and still is home to a lot of the peripheral bits of the film and television industries. Many of the world's major film companies have offices in or near Wardour Street, a stone's throw from the site of Conti's in my day. You'll also find audio studios, preview theatres, equipment hire services, in fact anything and everything you might need if you wanted to make a movie, with the exception, of course, of the money.

Me with Joan Ann Maynard in Never So Good

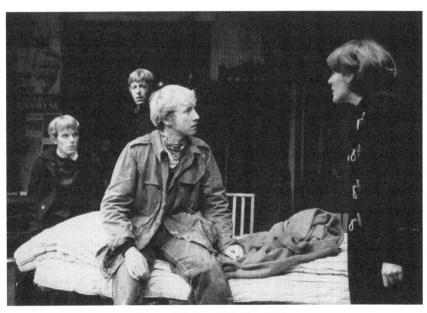

Me as Wick with Helen Weir

To a young aspiring actor being at the heart of things made it all feel a lot more real. Most people have very little contact with the world of entertainment except as part of the audience; in Soho we were surrounded by people involved in that world, so we felt involved in it too. I think that helped me and my fellow Conti-boys to stay focused; the one thing Conti's has probably never had is a discipline problem, because we all wanted to be there and to do well. Plus, of course, if you wanted to be naughty there was far more scope for misbehaviour outside the school gates than within them.

The decriminalisation of being gay, the ready availability of pornography on the internet and, I suspect, a desire to avoid upsetting the more prudish tourists have combined to rob Soho of much of its character. Back then you never knew quite who or what you might see and hear if you peered furtively through open doors into a smoky basement. There was a coffee bar called 2 i's (pronounced 'two-eyes') which I found especially attractive despite its having no naked ladies on display. For what it lacked in that respect it more than made up for in coolness. It billed itself as 'Home of the Stars' and was where you could go to hear Tommy Steel, who performed there regularly before he found fame and fortune. Ditto (the perhaps unfortunately named) Wee Willy Harris, Britain's 'wild man of rock 'n' roll'.

The café was sandwiched between a continental grocery and another coffee bar called Heaven and Hell where an espresso would have cost you nine old pence – just under 4p today. Those were the days!

Later on there was the Macabre Café which used fake coffins as tables, fake skulls as ashtrays and which did have naked ladies; albeit only wispy painted ones on the walls.

The area was not without its depressing side, though. Not far from the school was the headquarters of the Musicians' Union, which I think must also have acted as an agency for session players. In any event, one frequently saw down-at-heel characters with violin cases and the like under their arms going in and out of the place. I'd seen quite a few gangster movies by then, and I always wondered if the instruments were in reality Chicago typewriters (Thompson machine guns, as used by bootleggers etc. during the Prohibition era to discourage rival gangs, policemen etc) and the so-called Union a front for organised crime. Also nearby was a music shop called Boosey & Hawkes which was always fun to visit. If they weren't too busy they'd let you play on the drum-kits, until you started making too much noise of an unmusical nature, when they would throw you out.

Life was therefore hectic and demanding, and to relax my father and I would set off in his newly-acquired Hillman motor car to the village of Laleham, where he would cast me adrift on the Thames in an old tyre inner-tube. I used to worry that he expected me to float all the way to Battersea and that I'd be home too late for tea. That wasn't the only threat to my life, though; the Hillman also tried to kill me.

These days, car doors are designed in such a way that if they should open spontaneously while the vehicle is moving the rushing air tends to hold them closed. The Hillman's front doors were hung the other way, so that when mine flew open as we rounded a right-hand bend it was pushed fully open by the wind. This was in the days before seatbelts, and the only thing that stopped me falling out was the speed of my father's reaction; he managed to grab me with one hand and bring the car safely to a standstill. Most fathers would have been angry with me for not shutting the door properly, or would have complained to the people who sold him the car. Not my Dad; his solution was to go to the iron monger's where he bought a small but efficient brass bolt which he mounted on the Hillman's offending door. I still wonder how many of the Fleet Air Arm's Swordfish aircraft stayed aloft thanks to his inventiveness and ingenuity.

With Enid Blyton and Gloria Johnson as Silky

I was becoming something of a child star; the stream of work never seemed to dry up. One of the most demanding roles of my whole career was that of Enid Blyton's *Noddy* whom I played for two consecutive Christmas seasons in London, first at the Prince's

Theatre, then at the Victoria Palace. Noddy is a multi-faceted character, part cherub, part philanthropist and part boy-racer. I doubt if any child actor then or now could be expected to walk straight into the part. I had first to serve my apprenticeship by playing the Seller of Spells (and doubling as the Ticket Collector) at London's Stoll Theatre. We opened there a few days before Christmas 1956 and ran until the middle of January 1957, giving 24 Matinee performances. Also appearing was the then well-known entertainer Leslie Saroney who played a character called Mr Pinkwhistle. Mr Saroney was famous as the writer of a popular song called Ain't it Grand to be Blooming Well Dead? a question to which he presumably found the answer when he passed away in 1985 at the ripe old age of 88.

The 1956/7 production must have gone well – though I'm afraid I can barely remember it now – because the following year we moved to larger premises and I was promoted to play the title role. Miss Blyton liked my performance and re-employed me the following year.

Some Americans came and saw the show and evidently liked it, as they arranged for a performance to be filmed in its entirety for showing in the USA. It was my first (and so far my only) casting in the title role of a film, and that obviously entitled me to the full red-carpet treatment and loads of dosh. Obvious to all but the producers, that is. Still, even the paltry nineteen guineas they paid me seemed like a lot of money back then.

My old friend Graeme Harper played Moonface, a character which Blyton aficionados will recognise as an import from her *Faraway Tree* stories.

Graeme was to remain a friend for life and I've worked under his direction many times, notably in two series of *Doctor Who*. Looking at him now it's not too hard to remember the ginger-haired freckle-faced kid in short trousers who used to commute to Conti's from his home in Hertfordshire every day.

We took to each other immediately. He was and still is one of the most likeable people I have ever met, always willing to share his things, though that wasn't always a good thing. I remember once he had a bottle of combined after-shave and fake tan. He looked and smelt pretty good in it and I was delighted when he allowed me to try it. I don't think it was designed for people with my sort of skin, though, as it left me an evil-smelling blotchy mess, and it took me days to rid myself of it completely.

Graeme and I were both considered very good actors, though for some reason I seemed to get bigger and better parts than he did. Graeme nevertheless managed to earn his school-fees, and I often wonder if he was right to give up acting when he was still a very young man, recently married. His ambition was always to direct, and on leaving Conti's he was taken on by the BBC as a runner – something between an apprentice and an errand-boy. It wasn't long before they recognised his potential and sponsored his training, enabling him to become that rarity, an actor's director; one who listens to the cast and doesn't allow his own ego to get in the way of doing a good job. It's probably for that reason that he is so highly regarded by those of us who have worked with him on Doctor Who, of which more, as they say, anon.

Although he usually stuck to TV, I had the pleasure of working with him in a theatrical production a few years ago, in a play called *Schoolboy Blues*. The cast consisted of myself and about half a dozen other actors, including John Challis who is perhaps best known for playing the part of Boycie in the long-running BBC comedy series *Only Fools and Horses*. It was to be the inaugural production at a little theatre above the main bar of the Rose pub in Fulham Road, now, sadly, no more. Before its conversion and our arrival its large upstairs room had been used as a rehearsal space by several Masonic lodges, among them, it transpired, one attended by my then next-door neighbour. Fortunately his lodge was able to find an alternative venue without too much difficulty, so we remained friends. I had no hand in choosing the venue for our production, it was an extremely unlikely coincidence. However, if you find that hard to believe, try this; many years after I moved out of the house next to his, the landlady of the Rose retired and moved into it. They do say it's a small world, but I still can't quite believe that it's that miniscule.

CHAPTER THREE

A HINT OF FAME AND FORTUNE

It was when I played Noddy that I was first asked for my autograph. In fact it was expected that after the show I would make my way to the foyer, still in costume and 'full slap' i.e. make-up, to chat to members of the young audience and sign their autograph books. This was before the days when you could charge for signed photos, of course – something which nowadays provides much of my 'walking-around money'. I was also invited on to the BBC Home Service's regular Saturday evening chat show, *In Town Tonight*, with it's wonderful signature tune, Eric Coates' Knightsbridge March which was followed by a cry of 'Once more we stop the mighty roar of London's traffic …'

Looking back, I suppose that must have been my first ever live broadcast. There were to be many more. Before they had good quality video-tape a lot of TV programmes went out either completely live or with tele-cine and interlaced on-stage action. In those days the BBC was always courteous to young actors and I still have two very polite letters from them, one asking me to appear on the show and the other thanking me for having done so.

Talking of letters, I used to receive quite a lot of those from children who had come to see the show. I tried always to answer them in person, but if the writer had included a phone number it was always tempting to use it rather than writing. Doing so to one young fan led to my parents and me being invited to tea with his parents and older brother. They turned out to live in a rather grand house, separated from the nearest road by what seemed to me to be a very long drive. There was even a pair of electrically operated gates which opened for us when we arrived. We were greeted at the door by a butler who announced us to the family. The young fan concerned was delighted to see me, as, surprisingly, was his older brother, Christopher, who was much nearer my own age. Our parents also seemed to hit it off. In fact they became good friends, as did Christopher and I, to the extent that in our mid-teens we got into trouble together.

By then Chris' younger brother Timothy had passed away from the leukaemia from which he must have been suffering when I first met him, though I didn't know it at the time. Looking back, I wonder if my parents did know, and if that was the reason they went to the trouble of taking me out into the wilds of Surrey to meet him that day.

The trouble Chris and I got into wasn't too serious. The police fortunately weren't involved, and I hope they will agree that after nearly fifty years it's too late to prosecute me now. However, and just to be on the safe side, let us suppose, purely hypothetically, that two teenaged boys, one with a freshly-minted driving licence, the other still too young to obtain one, might have been left alone with no adult supervision and in close proximity to an attractive car, say, perhaps, a Singer Gazelle convertible. Its keys might have been in the ignition so they might have been tempted to take it for a spin – hypothetically. Imagine too that the slightly older one with the driving licence would probably yield to his young friend's insistence that he, with no licence, should be the one to drive, on the dubious grounds that it was his mother's car, not mine (oops, I mean "the older one's").

Oh, how inviting those country lanes might have been for two such dare-devils, and how skilful might the unlicensed younger one be at negotiating bends and avoiding the raised ironwork in the roadside gullies. Nasty things, raised drainage grilles, though. They have an annoying habit of encouraging cars to bounce off them then roll over a couple of times before ending up in the middle of the road with their wheels in the air and (in the case of open-topped vehicles) their erstwhile occupants a few yards behind them with all manner of newly-acquired bruises and abrasions.

In this entirely hypothetical scenario, neither young person would have worn a seatbelt, few cars were fitted with them and their use was not compulsory, otherwise the hypothetical outcome might have been far worse. That's not to say I don't think seatbelts are a good idea. In most cases they do save lives, and I'm forever telling my family to belt up.

Had any of this actually happened it might well have been necessary for friends and neighbours to rally round and ensure that the injured persons received medical assistance and that any potentially incriminating evidence in the form of inverted vehicles vanished from the scene of any (still purely hypothetical) accident.

All this would have happened (had it happened at all) several years after my stint as Noddy. I would by then have been appearing in a BBC TV schools programme called Television Club, and I'm sure you can imagine how upset the BBC might have been had one of their stars turned up at the studio bearing the scars of some illicit automotive adventure, and at the juggling of camera-positions that would have been necessary to avoid any accidental display of stitched-up eyebrows and severely-grazed hands. Not, of course that it ever happened, so there's no need to charge anyone with allowing themselves to be carried in a vehicle taken without consent, or conspiracy to pervert the course of justice … as someone who knows about these things tells me could have been the case.

Yet again, I digress. I was actually telling you about the Noddy years, the late 1950s. Enid Blyton was a delightful lady and always kind to us young actors. She told me on one occasion that I was the best Noddy she had ever seen. I hope and believe she meant it, but perhaps she said it to all of us.

She also thoroughly approved of the Evening News' charitable appeal; 'Toy for a Sick Child' as part of which I, dressed as Noddy and in full make-up, would visit children in hospital and hand out Noddy and Big Ears toys. I was allowed to keep a couple, I still have them. They're in (almost!) mint condition as I never played with them myself, and because they are precious to me I haven't allowed my own children or grandchildren to play with them either. Mean, I know, but they are for me a link to a bygone age, before I became really famous … which I did … Ask anyone sufficiently mature to recall the middle of last century if they remember me and they will probably only have to rack their brains for a day or two before responding, 'Wasn't he so-and so in such and such?' I probably was. As a child actor I appeared in a lot of things, and became a recognised 'face' from the telly, no doubt to the delight of the Agency part of Conti's who took a percentage of my earnings.

As Noddy delivering Christmas toys

In my mid-teens I starred as Dickon Sowerby in the BBC's eight-part adaptation of Frances Hodgson Burnett's *The Secret Garden* and as Peter in a children's TV drama called *Heidi*. In the original book, written by Johanna Spyri, the story was set in the Swiss Alps. For reasons of economy, though, the outdoor scenes were shot not in Andermatt or Zermatt but were filmed at Whipsnade Zoo in Bedfordshire.

Penshurst Place in Kent became the location for the exterior scenes in *The Secret Garden*. It was, and still is, a 14th century manor house. It has a long association with TV and film production, having served as a backdrop to various productions, from prestigious films such as *The Other Boleyn Girl* to dog food commercials.

The history of Penshurst is quite fascinating. It belonged originally to Henry VIII, whose son Edward VI gave it to Sir William Sidney, an ancestor of the present owner, in 1552 as a reward for some favour or other. I was not yet fifteen though, and neither knew nor greatly cared about the history of the place. I simply knew that it was inconvenient to get to, especially early in the morning. My character was a curly-haired Yorkshire lad; my own hair being stubbornly straight I had to spend a lot of time in curlers before filming could begin, thus the early starts.

I don't recall anything going terribly wrong at Penshurst, but then, unlike Whipsnade, it wasn't a zoo. There is an old theatrical adage: never work with animals or children. Joy Harrington, who directed and co-wrote the series, ought to have known better; taking a cast made up mostly of kids (including some very young goats) to film in a zoo was just asking for trouble. When it came, though, it was from a wholly unexpected source.

Me as Peter, and Sarah O'Conner as Heidi

Filming in those days was a much more complicated business than it is today. There was no autofocus, so cameramen used tape-measures to ensure the main characters weren't too fuzzy, and mistakes with the lighting could not easily be corrected once the shot was 'in the can'. Film was expensive to buy and processing it was both costly and slow. Given an already tight budget, foul-ups, no matter how funny, were not appreciated either by the director and producer or the bean-counters to whom they answered. Terry Wogan had yet to be invented, so there was no Auntie's Bloomers to make out-takes more cost-effective.

Thus it was probably only the younger members of the cast, unaware as we then were of the facts of (economic) life, who laughed when the filming of a particularly tricky scene was brought to a close, both dramatically and technically, just seconds before we had finished shooting it by Joy's exasperated cry of, 'CUT!!'

It had been a difficult scene to set up, not least because it involved more than a few goats. I was playing a juvenile goat-herder. I didn't have to do too much actual herding – there was someone called a goat wrangler who saw to all that – but I don't think the animals had read the script as they took ages to find their proper places. After what seemed like hours of hanging around waiting for them we finally got the scene under way, and it was all going fairly well until Joy's shout.

For a moment we were bewildered, wondering what we could have done wrong. We knew our lines and we hadn't bumped into the furniture; how could it be our fault? It was only when we followed Joy's finger to the horizon that we understood.

A mob of kangaroos, or they may have been wallabies, had bounced into the background. I think 'mob' is the right collective noun as it apparently works for either species of marsupial. I later found out that they had not, as I first thought, escaped from the zoo, but were part of a sizeable population of wallabies then living wild in the area. I think the goats must have been as startled as we were, as they all moved out of position and we had yet another long wait while the wrangler rounded them up, at the end of which we had a better understanding of Joy's annoyance and frustration.

My first major TV part was in 1958 when I played a lad called Ginge in what may have been the one of the first TV movies ever made. Running for an hour and shot in black-and-white, it was called *The Little Beggars*, written by Caryl Brahms and Ned Sherrin. It was shown on 20th March 1958 at half-past eight in the evening, and was a modern-day version of John Gay's *Beggars Opera,* which dating as it did from 1728, presumably had the advantage of being out of copyright. I've looked on the internet for our version but it seems to have vanished completely, and I can only assume it's been lost forever with no chance of a repeat-fee coming my way. Much the same can be said of other series I appeared in, such as *The Golden Spur* and *Ask for King Billy.* They may or may not have been great TV, but money is money.

Me with Donald Churchill

Perhaps I should say a few words about the way actors get paid. Badly, infrequently and grudgingly are the words that first spring to mind, but that's not quite what I mean. Generally speaking, you get a one off payment for film-work whereas for a 'telly' you get paid once for doing it then a (reducing!) percentage of your original fee each time it gets shown anywhere in the world. In the theatre, you keep your fingers crossed and hope that the ghost will walk.

In Shakespeare's *Hamlet* there is one character who has no lines to say, the ghost of Prince Hamlet's father, the late King Hamlet. Calling for little technical skill that role could safely be entrusted to the company manager, whose other duties traditionally included handing out the cast's wages each week. The perambulations of the spectre have thus from time immemorial been linked to that happy event. However, especially when you're touring, disappointments are not unknown; if you can't put enough bums on seats the production will fold and you'll be lucky to get your bus-fare home. It happened to me when I toured with Richard Murdoch and Charlie Drake in *The Happiest Days of Your Life*, but I'm getting ahead of myself – again!

Later that same year, 1958, I was working again for the BBC, playing a boy called Venables in a TV series called *Jennings at School,* adapted from Anthony Buckeridge's stories about boys at an English prep-school. So much work inevitably took its toll on my health. As days went by my throat became sore and my voice started to fade. For a television actor this was bad news, but at least some cunning deployment of microphones made the problem less noticeable. Doctors were summoned and palliative medicines administered by the bucket-load, or so it seemed to me.

Me as Venables on the left. John Mitchell as Jennings centre. Copyright BBC

However, there was another problem; I was due to start my second season as Noddy just a few days later, but I now had full-blown tonsillitis and surgery was required. Other kids who had the operation were given a fortnight off school to recuperate. No such luck for Noddy! For him it was off with the anaesthetic mask and on with the pointy-hat with the bell on it. The show had to go on ... OK, that might be a slight exaggeration. I see that it looks as though I was driven by ambulance from the recovery room to the stage door. Thinking back, it wasn't quite like that, it just felt as if it was.

It was while I was working on *Jennings* that I became friendly with the young actor who played the title role. John Mitchell was about three years my junior, but our parents had become friends and our two families spent a lot of time together at the Mitchells' home in Greenford. I suppose that like most teenaged boys I had reservations about befriending someone who had yet to attain teen status, though if the term 'teenager' had by then been invented it was certainly not as charged with meaning as it is today. Be that as it may, any reservations I had were easily outweighed by the access our friendship gave me to his drum kit, which was kept in the attic, well away from and (hopefully) out of earshot of both family and neighbours. I don't think I was all that bad at it, but it soon became obvious that I was nowhere near as good a drummer as young Mitch, as he was known, who was eventually to give up acting in favour of a career in music, though not before achieving considerable success in a number of comedy roles, including that of Peregrine Wendover in the British film *Bottoms Up*, starring the late 'Professor' Jimmy Edwards. One of Jimmy's more memorable and oft-repeated lines was 'Bend over, Wendover '.

I don't know if Mitch ever knew he was the second choice for that part. It had been offered to me first, but due to other commitments I was unfortunately unavailable. I say unfortunately, but I had read the script and in hindsight it may have been the frequency with which that line appeared on the pages and thus the prospect of all that whacking that made me turn it down. Not that I'm a coward when it comes to such things. I once appeared in a TV documentary about the legendary Streatham Madam, Cynthia Payne ... More about that later on.

By the age of twenty Mitch was a regular performer at several London jazz clubs, and after working with many well-known 1960s rock bands he went on to become the main drummer with a group called Georgie Fame and the Blue Flames. He subsequently became a founder-member of The Jimi Hendrix Experience, featuring on many ground-breaking numbers including the unforgettable *Purple Haze*, the master-tape of which had to be sent to Reprise Records for remastering and labelled with the warning message 'DELIBERATE DISTORTION. DO NOT CORRECT '.

Mitch and I remained friends until his untimely death in 2008.

Acting is a dangerous profession with a high risk of getting murdered, something which for a while in 1956 happened to me once or twice a day. I was at the Old Vic, playing the Earl of Rutland in *Henry VI Part 3*. My death was necessary to the plot, and so I had to go. The chosen weapon was a dagger, wielded as I recall by an actor called James Culliford, but to make sure the job was done properly the theatre designer had provided an alternative.

It might not have been just to make sure I died but in my youthful naïveté I assumed he thought the audience would be comprised of ankle fetishists, or that perhaps he just wanted to ensure the people in the front seats didn't miss any of the action. For whatever reason, the stage was higher at the back than at the front. I think they told me it was 'raked' but I thought that just meant that they'd got rid of the dead leaves on the grassy bits. Only later did I learn the truth, i.e. that most stages are similarly raked, and that actors just have to make allowances and put up with it.

Anything placed on a table would therefore have a tendency to slide off it, including one evening the apparently lifeless remains of yours truly. When I was placed on the table I tried to hold on, using all the strength I could muster which, bearing in mind I'd just been stabbed, probably wasn't much. I should tell you that retaining the

appearance and sound of a dead body when you fall a couple of feet
to land with a thud on a hard surface is not easy, and was not, as far
as I can recall, on the syllabus at Conti's.

The script called for me to be picked up and carried off stage by
Harold Innocent, who luckily was strong enough to lift me from the
floor. He did it with his customary aplomb and I doubt if anyone in
the audience ever suspected that it wasn't supposed to happen that
way.

Harold is probably one of those people you've seen on TV and in
films many times without really noticing him. He was that good! He
was equally at home as hero or villain. Perhaps if I mention his role
as the not-especially reverend Bishop of Hereford in the 1991 film
Robin Hood: Prince of Thieves starring Kevin Costner you might be
able to put a face to the name. Or as Sir George Baker, one of the
king's doctors, in the London production of Alan Bennett's *The
Madness of George the Third*. I, however, was not entirely happy about
the accident, and complained to the director, pointing out that I had
bumped my head and bruised my bottom when I fell. He was
unconcerned: in fact he even had the gall to suggest that we 'keep it
in'. Such is the dedication to one's craft expected of a young actor.

CHAPTER FOUR

TROUBLED TEENS ...

As a teenager I suffered some very bad treatment at the hands of grown-ups. I was threatened by an escaped convict and forced to steal food and other things for him. I was expected to spend time working for a mad old woman in her rather grand but frankly filthy home, where food from years ago still lay uneaten on the table. The old dear's clothes appeared not to have been changed since the aforementioned food was first laid out. For a while I put up with it because I had fallen desperately in love with the lady's adopted daughter, but she spurned my advances and I became increasingly miserable. When, perhaps inevitably, I got the sack I was forced instead to work each day in a small room which was dirty, noisy and far too hot, at the beck-and-call of a man who seemed intent on keeping me in poverty and degradation for several years.

Fortunately I was remembered in someone's will and suddenly found myself with more than enough money to get away from all that and make my way to London and the sort of life-style I felt was my due and which I enjoyed to the full, much to the disapproval of my elders and betters.

All this, of course, was an entirely vicarious experience; I was playing the part of Young Pip in the BBC's adaptation of Dickens' *Great Expectations*.

Me as Pip. Copyright BBC

Me as Pip with Gordon Rollings as Pumblechook. Copyright BBC

That was probably the part which gave my career its first real boost, far more so, I suspect, than playing Noddy because appearing on TV every week I was seen by millions rather than by mere thousands. On the other hand I might not have been selected to play Pip if I hadn't been Noddy. Who knows, but regardless of all that I was extremely lucky to get the part. The BBC had invited applications from every stage-school and talent agency in London. By then there were quite a lot: Corona, Ada Foster and several others. I think in the end I was chosen from some forty or fifty young hopefuls.

The escaped convict, Magwitch, was played by Jerold Wells, who although British by birth, moved to Australia at the age of eight when his parents died. He stayed there until after the Second World War; much of which he spent as a prisoner of the Japanese. Before his capture he had, as a member of an army theatrical company entertaining the troops, been part of a real-life version of the BBC's popular show *It Ain't Half Hot, Mum*. The role of Magwitch was his first major part in the northern hemisphere, but was followed by many more.

In the 1960s and 1970s he was often to be seen in sitcoms and other light entertainment programmes, notably as a regular guest on Benny Hill's (now somewhat notorious) TV Shows and with Messrs Corbett and Barker in *The Two Ronnies*.

There was nothing to laugh at in his Magwitch persona, though; children up and down the land were terrified of him. Even I was a little bit wary in his company, especially after one rehearsal when instead of grabbling me by the shirt-sleeve he helped himself to a handful of my arm. I remember it hurt, quite a lot, and left a lovely bruise. Fortunately he managed to get it right when we came to do the scene live.

Although some of the outdoor scenes were shot on the Isle of Sheppey in Kent others were filmed at Lime Grove, from where a programme called *Top of the Pops* was also broadcast. After work, I was sometimes able to join the audience, made up mostly of girls of about my own age.

Quite a lot of *Great Expectations* was done live, though, so a lot of effort had to go into making sure everything went smoothly on the night. For the actors this meant a lot of time spent learning lines. For the stage crew it meant meticulous attention to detail. Needless to say it didn't always work out as it should, and sometimes we had to improvise and ad lib our way out of trouble.

I still occasionally have nightmares about a scene with my beloved, the haughty and aloof Estella, played by Sandra Michaels, who a couple of years earlier had played Phyllis in *The Railway Children*; the TV series, not the film. She and I were ostensibly playing a card game called beggar-my-neighbour which I was supposed to lose. In those days, the late 1950s, it would still have been quite a popular game and many viewers would have been able to follow its progress, so it was important that the deck was stacked in the right order. Unfortunately on this occasion it wasn't. Sandra and I had no choice but to play on in the hope that the right cards would turn up. Time was slipping away though.

We had to be off-air before the news, which nothing was allowed to delay or interrupt, so I said something like, 'That's it! All my cards are plain so you have won this, Miss,' and we moved on. I couldn't swear to it and I don't suppose the viewers heard it, but I'm sure there were loud sighs of relief from the producer.

Me as Pip, and Sandra Michaels as Estella. Copyright BBC

The Cover of Radio Times April 1959

Great Expectations was a major BBC production and received a lot of publicity. It made the cover page of the Radio Times, with a large picture of me, which made my mother very proud indeed, so much so that I think she bought every available copy from our local newsagent.

My career was not going entirely smoothly at this time; parts were not being handed to me on a plate.

I remember being very excited when I was asked to take a screen-test for the part of Ransome, the cabin boy, in a forthcoming Walt Disney production of Robert Louis Stevenson's *Kidnapped*, and then very disappointed when they decided to use someone else.

I haven't been able to find out who it was. It might have been either a young American actor called Richard Evans (I say 'young' but he was in his twenties, which is probably knocking on a bit for a cabin boy) or a slightly younger actor called John Pike. Whoever it was, I dare say I tried to blight his career with curses, as teenagers are wont to do when others deprive them of what they feel is rightfully theirs. If I did then I don't think I succeeded. Mr Evans had a reasonably successful and probably very financially rewarding career in both film and television, appearing in *Wagon Train, Gunsmoke, Alfred Hitchcock Presents, Star Trek* and many other well-known shows, but is probably best remembered as high-school teacher Paul Hanley in the long-running and, for its time, scandalously salacious soap opera *Peyton Place.*

The same source, however, shows no credits for John Pike after 1965 when he starred with Steve Marriott (of whom more anon) in an American film called *Be My Guest,* but whose entry on another website tells me that in 1971 he (and I quote) 'began his career as a disc jockey and later moved into TV news, holding various positions from anchor-man to programming executive at a series of stations in Florida, Massachusetts and Ohio. He made the move to the networks in 1980 when he was named vice president of program development for the NBC TV Stations Division, with responsibilities for sports and children's programming as well as late-night scheduling.' Where would we be without the internet?

It would seem, then, that whichever of them played that cabin boy did very well for himself, but should he ever read this, I would like him to know that I have forgiven him for pinching my part and bear him no malice or ill will. Well, not very much, anyway. It was, after all, a long, long time ago.

In 1961 I worked on a children's TV serial called *Stranger on the Shore,* the story of a young French au-pair girl's arrival and stay in Brighton. Acker Bilk's song *Jenny*, named in honour of his daughter, was adopted as the signature tune and subsequently released as a single called ... well, I'll let you guess! Mr Bilk came along to our recordings and was introduced to the cast. From then on we sometimes went to listen to him when he appeared at various trad-jazz clubs. I still quite like that sort of jazz, but I'm afraid I can't be doing with much of the modern stuff. Thelonious Monk, Miles Davis, Herbie Hancock, John Coltrane and all that lot leave me cold.

CHAPTER FIVE

SNAKES AND LADDERS

I don't think I was ever meant to be a film star. I don't know why. I had the looks, the voice and the talent. Perhaps it was all down to other people pinching my parts. It certainly happened more than once.

In 1962 I was lucky enough to be offered the part of Eric Sykes and Miriam Karlin's eldest son in *Heavens Above*, a Boulting Brothers comedy made at Shepperton Studios and starring Peter Sellers. I duly turned up, and spent a few very enjoyable weeks working with more-or-less the whole upper echelon of British acting talent; in no particular order, people such as Ian Carmichael, William Hartnell, Bernard Miles, Miriam Karlin, Roy Kinnear, Joan Hickson, Derek Nimmo, the catalogue goes on and on. If you look it up you'll see the full list.

Unfortunately, you won't find my name amongst them, not even as 'Uncredited'! That's because there was a bit of a mix up. When I was supposed to be called to do my one big scene as 'Jack', they called for Steve Marriott by mistake. At least, that was his story; I'm not saying money changed hands, and Steve and I remained friends up to and after his change of career. He became lead singer with The Small Faces and subsequently of a group called Humble Pie. Once Steve had left, the former group was joined by Ronnie Wood and Rod

Stewart, and as they were considerably taller than the rest of the group the word 'Small' was dropped from their name. Until then I'd always assumed the name referred to the sizes of their boat races; Cockney rhyming slang for 'faces'. Forgive me, I'm an expert on the subject. I even give lectures ... well, sort of.

I therefore had very little to do on set. I was definitely there, though and if you watch very carefully you'll see me on screen several times. As there are no repeat fees involved I won't be upset if you don't. Neither do I think Steve owed me anything for usurping my part.

I used to spend quite a lot of time at the flat he shared with the rest of the Faces. Perhaps he had an aversion to launderettes, or maybe he had a position as a fashion icon to maintain, but one of his foibles was that he never wore an item of clothing more than once. Consequently, the corner of his room often played host to a pile of discarded garments, all destined for the dustbin, should he ever get round to taking them there. This seemed to me to be inordinately wasteful, and I was very glad to receive his invitation to help myself to whatever I wanted. His taste in clothes was similar to my own i.e. impeccable, and my wardrobe grew considerably. I wish I still had some of them. They'd be worth a fortune!

My somewhat reduced role in *Heavens Above* meant that I had time on my hands, but Shepperton Studios is a good place to pass a few hours in idleness. There were occasional games of cricket, which Peter Sellers would quite often join in. He was great fun to be around, and though I think we were all a bit in awe of his glamourous life-style, not to mention his Ferrari and his customised Mini with the wicker-basket doors, he turned out to be perfectly friendly and approachable. Then there was my new toy to be played with, a magnificent Vespa scooter on which I used to travel to the studios each day. I would also ride it round and round the studios, occasionally, I admit, pretending to myself that it was a Norton or a Harley-Davidson.

There were always several films being made at Shepperton. One day my friend Greg Phillips, another Conti boy who happened to be working on the next-door sound-stage, starring with Dirk Bogarde in a film called *I Could Go On Singing*, introduced me to a rather attractive young lady of about my own age whose mother was working on the same movie. In the course of the next couple of weeks I managed to persuade her, the daughter that is, not the mother, to accompany me on several of my impromptu tours of the back lot. I may not have a claim to fame for my part in the film, but I think I have one for that. How many other people do you know who've carried Judy Garland's daughter, Liza Minnelli, on the pillion of their scooter?

I wouldn't work in film again until I played a soldier called Alf in *Before Winter Comes*, a rather harrowing story about life in a post-war refugee camp released in 1969 and starring David Niven, of which more anon, but though my film career may not have been a roaring success, if you switched on a television set at almost any time of the day or evening throughout the 1960s there was a strong chance that I would be in whatever came on. Bear in mind, though, that in the early part of that decade there were only two channels, and they closed down at about eleven o'clock in the evening.

One of the first things I did in that decade was a six-part serial for Associated Rediffusion called *A Brother for Joe*, in which I played a character called Roddy. The director was Vladek Sheybal, a former member of the Polish Resistance who had survived two periods of incarceration in a Nazi concentration camp. Better remembered now as an actor, he was something of a perfectionist as a director and made quite an impression on younger members of the cast. I came to regard him as a mentor. I think it was he who insisted that 'Actors can do *anything*!' meaning that apart from acting, singing and dancing you had to master skills as diverse as cooking and bare-back riding.

A Brother for Joe. Me with Penny Watts

I was perhaps especially fortunate, therefore, to have been selected to appear in a number of training films for the armed forces. The first and perhaps most demanding was for the Royal Navy, when I learnt to find my way into a dry-suit. You start by putting your feet through the neck, and it involves a lot of wriggling and jiggling, hilarious for spectators but not so funny for the would-be diver.

I played a sailor undergoing training as a diver and was one of a small group of actors working on the film. Before we could go to sea and do real diving we had to do some basic training at a shore-establishment, HMS Daedalus, I think it was called. The dry suits we were using came with a little bottle of compressed air, a bit like the ones you can buy for sealing punctured bike and car tyres but without the gooey gunge. The idea was that when you reached a certain depth and the pressure on the suit was so great that you couldn't move your arms and legs properly you pressed the button and sent air into the suit, forcing it away from your skin.

Getting in and out of those suits was quite tiring so once during a break in filming the rest of the cast and I decided to relax in the warm sunshine, still in our dry-suits. One of us (and he may be relieved to learn that I can't remember his name) relaxed to the point of dozing off, and after a few minutes was snoring gently. It was too good an opportunity to miss

I crept up on him and pushed the button. The result was spectacular. He immediately took on the proportions of a beached whale and started using language so blue as to make some passing (real) sailors blush. For several minutes he was rendered completely helpless, unable to stand or even to move whilst his loyal friends and colleagues lapsed into such violent hysterics as to render us equally incapable.

My character managed to complete his basic training as a frogman, fortunately without drowning or actually turning green. Unfortunately the same can't be said of the actor playing our instructor. He proved that he could turn very green indeed when, having completed the shore-based part of our training, the Navy took us out to sea on a minesweeper. If you've ever read Nicholas Monsarrat's novel *The Cruel Sea* you'll know how smooth and comfortable such craft were and understand why shooting some of the instructor's scenes took so long. It was because he suffered very badly from sea sickness and couldn't act for more than a minute or so before having to go and lean over the side. Eventually the director decided that restarting each time was just too expensive in terms of wasted film so he ordered that the camera be left running, no matter how revoltingly embarrassing that might have been for the poor man. At least in those halcyon days before YouTube he was spared the public humiliation which would nowadays be inflicted on him. The director then left it to post-production people to edit out the barf-breaks.

Even more fun to make though was a film called *Catt's Nine Lives*, in which the Navy taught me how to blow things up.

There is something very satisfying about watching things disappear with a very loud bang. Because we weren't really in the Service it was all rather informal when the camera wasn't rolling, so I didn't have to call the officer in charge, a Lieutenant Commander no less, 'Sir', addressing him instead by his nickname, which I seem to recall was 'Shiner' though I have no idea how he came by it.

During a break in shooting I happened to mention to him that I enjoyed sea fishing. We were on an army firing range on a beach near Dungeness. After asking me a few questions about my preferences for tackle and bait he fished a grenade out of his pocket, pulled the pin and lobbed it into the sea. A few seconds later there was a deafening explosion, and a lot of dead fish floated to the surface. Evidently pleased with the outcome he turned to me and said 'Now that's the way to fish …'

I received further training in the uses and abuses of explosives some years later, when I played the part of a safe-cracker in ITV's *The Bill*, working with gelignite. I suspect it wasn't the real McCoy. It occurred to me that I now had a new string to my bow should I find myself 'resting' for an extended period. I didn't turn to crime, though, and I've never really had to use my expertise in either diving or blowing things up, unless you count cleaning the pool at my Dad's villa in Spain or letting off a few fireworks in the back garden.

I did say you might have seen me on the telly at almost any time of the day or evening, and whilst back in the 1960s there was no real 'day-time' television in the modern somewhat pejorative sense of that phrase, programmes were broadcast throughout weekday mornings and afternoons, many of them aimed at schools.

One such was *Television Club*, a successor to a radio series called *The Jacksons* which was aimed at less able children, its aim being to help its audience develop the skills they would need to cope with everyday life events and problems.

I joined the programme in 1962 to play a character called Cliff Wade. The club used to 'meet' in an educational television studio at BBC Television Centre, and our host was a former teacher called Windsor Davies, who later found fame, and probably fortune, as Battery Sergeant Major Williams in *It Ain't Half Hot, Mum*. Our *Television Club* was intended for remedial classes and thus needed a rather milder, less military approach, which Windsor managed very well.

Central to each weekly instalment was a fifteen minute film featuring the family and their activities. I think the first one we did was about a train journey and focused on how to buy tickets and find the right platform. That, of course, was in the days when you simply bought a ticket from the British Railways ticket office at the station you were travelling from, without all the bother of shopping online to find the cheapest deal on offer from Heaven knows how many different franchises and agencies.

As time went by we moved on to more interesting and/or adventurous activities. I remember keeping pets, photography and seeing how they build a diesel-electric locomotive featured at various stages. Windsor would introduce the film, and afterwards he'd explain in more detail.

The Wade Family: Me as Cliff, Jean Alexander as Mum,
Bernard Kay as Dad and Linda Grange as Janet

It was a great series to be involved in, and some very well-known actors were involved. My screen mother was played by Jean Alexander, better known in those days as *Coronation Street*'s Hilda Ogden and later as the grasping shopkeeper Auntie Wainwright in *Last of the Summer Wine*. My character's sister Janet was played by a young actress called Linda Grange. Bernard Kay played my father in the first series; the part was taken over by Jimmy Beck who went on to play the spiv, Private Walker, in the original version of *Dad's Army*. Linda seems to have given up the acting profession not long after our second series. Bernard went on to feature in a number of films, notably *Doctor Zhivago*, and television programmes.

It was all good fun, but it was nevertheless another of those occasions when they tried to kill me. In one of the last episodes I ever did, they decided to teach me how to paddle a canoe. The location they chose was a place called Symonds Yat on the River Wye. The film was aired in June 1963, but I think we must have shot it rather earlier in the year because, as I was to discover to my cost, the water was very, very cold.

All went well until they got to the bit where I had to learn to right my canoe after capsizing. I managed it without assistance, which was probably just as well as none seemed to have been on offer, but was left coughing, spluttering and on the verge of acute hypothermia. Once the cameras had stopped I was handed a warm blanket and a cup of tea but little or no sympathy. I thought for one dreadful moment I was going to have to do it all over again when the sound technician told me he hadn't managed to record everything. Fortunately there was only one small bit missing: would I, he asked, please 'shiver again, for sound?'

Throughout the 1960s I worked with some very big names; Sybil Thorndike in a Saturday Playhouse production called *A Matter of Age*, David Kossoff and Peggy Mount in *The Larkins*, Frankie Howerd in his eponymous show, Bill Fraser and Irene Handl in Barry Took and Marty Feldman's comedy *Barney is My Darling*, Richard Vernon and Michael Aldridge in *The Fellows*, Benny Hill and Frank Thornton in *The Vanishing Man*, Wilfred Pickles in *Yorky;* once again the list goes on ...

Working with Dame Sybil Thorndike, who had by then been recognized as one of the theatrical greats for about 40 years, was a great privilege for a young actor, though I wonder looking back if my sixteen-year-old self fully appreciated that at the time. Again, I can remember very little about the production, but both Dame Sybil and her husband, Sir Lewis Casson, were delightful people and a joy to be around.

I spent so much time at the then brand-new Television Centre that I practically grew up in Wood Lane, though I also worked in the theatre, notably the Royal Court Theatre in Sloane Square, Chelsea. That particular venue had something of a reputation for putting on plays which sailed rather closer to the wind than most. We are talking of the days before the internet made images of almost everything people could do with, to or for each other accessible to just about everyone in the world. In those days there were still many who considered the mini-skirt rather shocking, the contraceptive pill was not available to unmarried women and any hint of a sexual act between men was illegal. Rumour used to have it that the only reason lesbianism *was* legal was that Queen Victoria found it so unlikely that ladies could indulge in such behaviour that she saw no point in

Me with Barry Evans in Spring Awakening

All plays intended for public performance were subject to censorship, the word of the Lord Chamberlain being, in all cases, law. Thus a play which explored different aspects of sexuality and/or called for the actors to pretend to do unmentionable things on stage must have been extremely lucky to survive that worthy's scrutiny. I appeared in one such play, *Spring Awakening*, at the Royal Court Theatre in 1965; I will say no more about it other than to stress that I really was pretending.

As a fairly well-known young actor in the 1960s I was also reasonably well-paid, something which caused pound signs to appear in the eyes of theatrical agents. Ten percent of a lot is much better than ten percent of not very much. One of the most successful agents of that time was a man called Al Parker (not to be confused with the American gay porn star!) and he was very keen to represent me.

Being part of his stable was a bit of a status symbol in those days, and I accepted with alacrity. After all, he had most of the major talents of the day on his books and they got a lot of work. Helen Mirren, James Mason and lots, lots more. He probably had too many prominent young hopefuls on his books, though, as nothing seemed to come my way. I gave it a couple of months and then asked to be released from my contract, which he was prepared to agree to.

Agents, I have come to believe, are fair-weather friends. If you're getting work they treat you like royalty; delicacy precludes me from saying what they treat you as when you're not. You can't really blame them, I suppose. Ten percent of nothing is effectively less than nothing. Resting actors can be a drain on the hospitality budget and are best dispensed with if they don't buck their ideas up. I'm sure that my current agent, who really couldn't be more helpful or work any harder on my behalf, isn't like that (whoever he or she might be at the time you read this).

I really enjoyed working in theatre, meeting many rising stars in the process. In 1964, for example, I appeared at St. Martin's Theatre, later home to the long-running London production of Agatha Christie's *The Mousetrap*, in a stage-adaptation of David Benedictus' novel *The Fourth of June* with the, sadly late, Simon Ward, well before he found fame as the eponymous hero of the film *Young Winston* in 1972.

It may be because it has been around for so much longer than TV and film but theatre seems to have a much richer store of traditions, myths and superstitions associated with it than Facebook, Instagram, YouTube and the rest. I suppose one day even so-called 'social media' will acquire their own set of such things, but I doubt they will be as interesting or enduring as the ones that surround stage work. I think I might take this opportunity to tell you a bit about the folklore and perhaps explain some of the jargon we actors use. I shall probably make myself slightly unpopular with my fellow Thespians for calling it that. If you are one of them please feel free to skip the next few pages.

Why 'Thespians', you might ask? Well, as I said, people have been acting on stages in front of live audiences for a very long time. Film, television and radio have been around for less than a hundred and fifty years, at the time of writing, but the first actor to portray a character other than himself on what may or may not have been a stage was, according to Aristotle, a man called Thespis, and he did it about 2600 years ago. That was even before Michael Billington took on the job of drama critic for the *Guardian* newspaper. The chances are Thespis had never been to drama school and didn't have an Equity card. The Equity card is something which was until fairly recently a prerequisite for anyone starting out as an actor. Nowadays though, membership of the actors' trade union is not compulsory and the profession is open to all. I applaud this, and in order to help newcomers to the world of entertainment on their way I will offer a little bit of advice.

First and foremost, probably the most important thing you can learn as an actor is your lines. I am by no means the first to say that, though, and I can't be sure the late Sir Noel Coward, actor and playwright, was either, when in 1954 he wrote: 'The only advice I ever give actors is to learn to speak clearly, to project your voice without shouting – and to move about the stage gracefully, without bumping into people. After that, you have the playwright to fall back on – and that's always a good idea.'

Contrary to popular opinion he didn't actually mention the furniture. That was a later substitution designed to make it funnier, but it is also sound advice, particularly if you're on a TV set like that used in the 1960s soap *Crossroads*. Bump into anything there and it was likely to fall down, over or both. I would add that no matter how well you know the play, your own lines and other people's, it's still vital that you listen to everything that's said and are prepared to steer things back on track if someone else goes wrong. It might be that another actor says something or perhaps asks a question out of turn. Imagine a detective questioning you in the role of suspected killer. He's supposed to ask you where you were on the night of the murder, to which you're supposed to reply that you were watching telly with some mates. He's then supposed first to ask you for your friends' names, then inquire as to what you were watching. Suppose he accidentally reverses those questions?

DI Smith: Which mates were those?

Suspect: Judge John Deed and Sherlock Holmes.

See the problem? Listen. And keep listening ...

Another important thing to learn is the difference between left and right. How can that be difficult? You need to remember two things; first, theatre directors do their job from in front of the stage, and second, that they expect you to do as you're told. If you're rehearsing a particularly complex scene, and especially if dancing or fighting are involved, the director might well shout out something on the lines of,

'Colin, could you move a couple of paces to the left as you're saying that?' and ever keen to please, you comply. Except that as far as he's concerned, you've moved to the right. He's looking from the front, don't forget. To avoid this confusion he should have said,

'… move a couple of paces *stage right* as you're saying that?'

Stage right and stage left mean to the right or left from the actor's point of view. If you move 'stage left' the audience sees you as moving to the right, and vice versa. I hope that helps; it's all very confusing and it can be quite difficult for young actors to grasp, especially if at the same time they're trying not to bump into the furniture.

If, like me, you are a polite and considerate actor, you will come to appreciate that one of the greatest sins you can commit in a theatre is to 'up-stage' another member of the cast, especially if that person's character is, in your opinion, of less importance than your own. Just as stages have a left and a right, they also have an up and a down. Almost all 'proscenium' stages are raked so that the audience can see all the actors' ankles no matter where they stand, and the stage slopes towards the audience. To move up-stage is to move away from the audience. Do that while someone is speaking to you and that person has little alternative but to turn his back on the punters and look at you while you're speaking. Anything else would appear both rude and a bit artificial. The audience therefore focuses their attention on the actor whose face they can still see. That is what is meant by up-staging someone, and it is very, very rude. Try not to do it. You will be nobody's darling if you do. No names, no pack-drill, but a certain comedian was notorious for using the trick.

There are many sources of possible disaster in a theatre, though slightly fewer these days than there were back in the days before electric lighting. You've heard of 'footlights', especially if you attended Cambridge University, and you will know that these were lights conveniently placed along the front of the stage where they could quite easily be kicked or trodden on, and which had the added advantage of adding years to an actor's apparent age by casting weird shadows to accentuate wrinkles, double chins and the like.

Footlights being a two-syllable word and therefore a little bit complicated, we actors tended to refer to them instead as 'floats'. There have been several different types of footlight used over the years, but our slang term is derived from what was probably the most primitive and potentially dangerous of them all, especially for anyone wearing floor-length inflammable costumes, wicks floating in oil or molten wax. Lighting from the front and sides being now much more controllable these days, floats rarely feature in modern productions, and it may be that a certain Cambridge institution will have to choose a new name.

Another good idea is to make sure you have wound up your watch because another terrible thing you can do is to turn up too late. Management generally likes you to be in the theatre before what is known as 'the half' i.e. thirty minutes before the five minute call. Some people will cut it fine, but I try to be in the theatre and getting ready at least an hour before the show. It gives me time to focus, to cope with any problems with make-up or costume and just generally to get into acting mode. Every dressing room has a loudspeaker, usually called the Tannoy though not necessarily made by that company.

Warning: do not rely on it!

Getting on and off stage at the right time is the actor's responsibility, and 'nobody told me' is *not* an acceptable excuse. As a matter of courtesy you will hear calls for the half, for fifteen and five minutes, and finally 'beginners'. The latter is not a call for novice actors to come down for a lesson. It means the people who are first on stage should already be waiting in the wings, the bits at the back and side of the stage people wander on and off through.

Assuming for a moment that you manage to arrive in plenty of time, avoid setting yourself or the theatre on fire, or bringing the house down, literally or figuratively, by bumping into things or people, the next worst thing that can happen is that you 'dry', that is, you forget your lines.

It happens to all of us at some time, and, paradoxically, the risk probably increases if you're in a long run. Say the same lines every day and twice on Saturdays for a few months and see if you can stop yourself turning on the autopilot, that wonderful built-in mechanism which enables you mentally to compile your shopping list for the day after you win the lottery whilst still acting your part convincingly. Then it happens; you come crashing back to reality and don't know where you've got to. Or someone who's been similarly daydreaming feeds you a wrong prompt. Whatever the cause, you're there, centre stage, the air crackling with dramatic tension, the audience sitting in hushed expectation of something really earth-shattering ... and you find you haven't a clue what you're supposed to say next!

Fortunately help is, or should be, at hand in the person of the DSM, the Deputy Stage Manager. Among that worthy's numerous duties is that of prompter. He or she will be sitting in a little booth out of sight of the audience and just a little bit to your left. Traditionally, prompters have always been placed 'stage left' (see above), but a 'bastard prompt' is not a DSM who feeds you the wrong line on purpose, but a prompter positioned stage *right*. There are some theatres, mostly newer ones, laid out that way, but nobody really knows why. I suppose, though, that if a prompter were to be a bit of a so-and-so he or she might have every justification because it is a very complex job, and the last thing a DSM needs is to have to mollycoddle a forgetful Falstaff or a tongue-tied Timon. DSMs have also to ensure that all cues, lighting, sound or whatever, happen at the right time, so that any electrical equipment such as radios, electric fans, dishwashers (the days of kitchen-sink drama being now more or less forgotten) and so on work at the right time.

Talking of prompts, there's a lovely story told of two elderly actresses who, together on stage, both simultaneously 'dried'. After a couple of seconds the DSM gave them a prompt, which he whispered in the usual way. Nothing happened; they both stood there, immobile and saying nothing. He tried again, a little louder. Same thing again. And again. Finally, as he was on the verge of tearing his hair out, one of the two ladies made her way across to his booth. 'We know the line, dear, but which one of us *says* it?'

Finally, a word or two about stage fright, which can be a terrible thing, and is nowhere near as rare as some in my profession would have you believe. The problem is that showing it is just not the 'done thing'; upper lips are supposed to remain stiff and the slightest sign of fear could mark you down as potentially unreliable.

I've always found it to be at its worst on opening nights. Never mind that I know my lines backwards, forwards and inside out, and that everything has been rehearsed to the point that I could play the part in my sleep, that first appearance before a live audience of paying punters still strikes terror in my heart. I have a theory that the true professional is not the one who doesn't suffer from stage fright but the one who gets on and does the job despite the anxiety.

Even so, nerves can still affect your performance, no matter how much starch you might apply to your upper lip. On the first night of *Present Laughter* my character Fred, Garry Essendine's valet, had to cross the stage carrying a tray with an empty cup and saucer on it. There may well have been milk, sugar and a teapot as well, but I can only remember that wretched cup and saucer. My hands were shaking slightly, so the crockery rattled, and to my ears that seemed to be very loud. The more conscious of the noise I became, the more my hands shook, and the louder it became. I thought I must be in danger of deafening the audience.

Yes, I know in hindsight that a rattling cup and saucer is unlikely to approach the threshold of pain, which someone told me is 110 decibels, so quite loud, but you don't always think logically in situations like that. I managed, somehow, to make it across the stage and exit through the door to Essendine's bedroom, but it was very worrying and even though first-night nerves would presumably not affect me on the second night I still thought something ought to be done about it.

That is what stage managers are for. I told ours about my problem and the next night the tray was covered with a cloth. Silence may not be golden, but it certainly calms the nerves.

From the above you may by now have gathered that to be a stage actor is to live dangerously, and that performing in front of a live audience in a theatre is potentially far more terrifying than film or television work, especially these days when most TV dramas are recorded in advance allowing embarrassing mistakes to be edited out or re-shot. The only real risk is that your catastrophic out-take will haunt you forever because some wag thought it would be a good idea to upload it to YouTube.

I don't know if actors really are more superstitious than most, but there are quite a few taboos which have been preserved over so many generations that it would be hard not to believe there was something in them. You should never, they say, refer to Shakespeare's *Macbeth* by name whilst in a theatre. You ought not to wish an actor good luck on a first night, and you must never ever whistle anywhere near a stage. Some of them have plausible, though not necessarily factual, explanations. The story goes that about ten years before we lost the American colonies an actor called Samuel Foot, desperate to obtain a licence for his Little Theatre, made a point of befriending, some might say 'sucking up to', the then Duke of York, in whose gift such licences lay. The two were hunting together, and Mr Foot fell off his horse, fracturing his femur. It was obviously very painful, and the Duke, perhaps feeling slightly guilty for having caused the accident, gave in and granted him the licence. The result was that we now have not the Little Theatre but the Theatre Royal in Haymarket, not far from Trafalgar Square. Does that reflect more befriending/sucking up? Be that as it may, 'Break a leg' has been the phrase of choice for wishing actors good luck on a first night ever since.

Alternatively, there was once an understudy, desperate to prove that he was every bit as good an actor as his starring principal, who half-jokingly said 'Break a leg!' to the man as he was about to go on. Somehow, I know not how, the man did break a leg, and the understudy took over for the rest of the run. Good luck for him, if not for his principal. True or false? Yer pays yer money and yer takes yer choice …

There is some evidence to suggest that whistling near a stage might once have been very dangerous indeed, especially if the production involved people or things flying around on ropes, or scenery dropping into place from above. Both would require complex rigging, and who better to arrange that than sailors? In the days before steam ships, crew were accustomed to climbing up masts and hoisting or lowering sails in response not to voice commands which might easily have been drowned out by crashing waves, cannon-fire or the cook's singing, but to whistles. Responding to a whistled signal was probably almost a reflex action for the sailors employed in theatres, so it might well have been very dangerous to whistle in a theatre. Anything and everything might have fallen on to you or someone else from a great height.

The reason *Macbeth* enjoys a somewhat macabre reputation and is traditionally referred to only as *The Scottish play* in theatres is, according to some, that on its first night, a very long time ago of course, an actor was killed on stage during a fight scene. It is said that a real dagger had been substituted for the fake one which should have been used. Other more complicated explanations abound, many involving witchcraft, real or imagined. Even if you think it's complete twaddle, though, you should out of politeness refrain from uttering the Scottish King's name inside a theatre, if only out of respect for the many actors who don't regard the taboo as superstitious nonsense.

Theatres being such dangerous places you may not be surprised to hear that many are said to be haunted. Some ghosts are more welcome than others, especially the ones that walk because they tend to bring the actors' wages with them. Others are believed to be malevolent, and have to be placated and treated with respect and consideration. The Palace Theatre in London keeps two seats in the balcony for their resident ghosts, fearing that their production would otherwise be cursed. I'm not sure if they tell the people in adjacent seats why that pair has been left empty, but if you should find yourself sitting by two vacant seats in that theatre, take care …

The idea of departed actors hanging around in theatres in the hope of re-living, if that's the word, past triumphs is quite common. You may know that theatres never actually close when a production ends, they simply 'go dark'. What you may well not know, though, is that the darkness is not total. One light, usually a single bulb placed centre stage, is always left on; called the 'ghost light' it is there to illuminate any posthumous productions the various spectres might stage.

Much as I love theatre, television was my main source of income through most of the 1960s. I worked with some very popular and well-established figures, people like Wilfred Pickles, then a very well-known actor and 'wireless' presenter. He was perhaps best known for hosting a radio show called *Have a Go*, which may well have been the first quiz show on British radio to give away money. Once, in 1953, the rollover main prize reached as much as £1 18s 6d (about £1.92). Remember though, that the average wage for a man in Britain at that time was less than £10 per week. Oh, to have today's income and yesterday's prices!

Have a Go was broadcast live from factories, village halls, or more or less anywhere the BBC could persuade people to gather and watch their friends, neighbours or colleagues talking about themselves and then answering four questions to win up to ten shillings (50p). If they were successful they also had a chance at the jackpot.

Me as Bobby with Wilfred Pickles as Yorky and Mary Mackensie

However, when I worked with Wilfred in 1960 it was in a TV series called *Yorky*. Wilfred played a schoolmaster and I a lad called Bobby Bennett. I can't remember much about it, except that as a young smoker I was very impressed by Mr Pickles' custom-made cigarettes, each of which bore his name. They must have been expensive, but he was nevertheless quite generous with them. I remember thinking those cigarettes were pretty cool and wishing I could have some made with my name on them, but I never did and as I have long-since given up the habit I doubt I ever shall. I told a friend of my ambition though; he suggested I change my name to 'John Player' to achieve the same result at less cost.

Wilfred must have liked my work as I was invited back a year or so later to play a young lad called Peter Macool in an episode called *The Student Teacher*. On that occasion I worked with a young man called Frazer Hines. I dimly remember travelling home with him by train, it might even have been pulled by a steam locomotive, it was that long ago, and spending much of the time playing cards with him. I have a vague feeling we might have been playing for money, and that I hoped to reduce him to betting his cowboy boots and losing them to me, but unfortunately I wasn't that good at poker (or bridge, canasta, whist, pontoon or even snap for that matter, and I'm no better now!) and I had to go for the better part of fifty years without owning a pair. It's a style of footwear we both seem to like though. Together in Texas a little while ago Frazer and I each bought a pair.

These were my teenage years and those of my early adult life, and as they were quite a long time ago now it may not surprise you to learn that my memories of them are perhaps a little hazy, nor that I'm probably not telling you everything that happened to me in those days.

With telly fame came the delights and risks of being recognised in the street. Sometimes it even became quite frightening. I remember once appearing at the Variety Club's *Star Gala* in Battersea Park, in 1969. There were many stars there that day; Tony Blackburn, Ray Barrett, Ron Moody, Liz Fraser and Roy Kinnear to name but a few. Now known simply as Variety, the charity funds activities for many disadvantaged children. You've probably seen their Sunshine coaches taking kids around the country. Frazer Hines and I were walking away from the stage area, probably, knowing us, intent on finding a pub, when we were noticed by a group of rather too many young ladies.

Being recognised by the odd one or two people is a delight. Having to hide from a pack of teenage girls who have spotted you in Battersea Park rather less so. It was the late 1960s and to be young, famous and male was to risk losing items of clothing to infatuated young fans. Having no wish to end up in that sort of trouble we took to our heels and managed somehow to outrun them before finding somewhere to hide, namely the ticket office for the Big Wheel, one of Battersea Funfair's major attractions. The cashier, seeing our predicament, took pity on us; whether or not she recognised either of us I couldn't say, but at least she didn't charge us for sheltering under her counter.

However, some aspects of a young man's life are perhaps best treated with discretion, and out of respect for those who helped me through that difficult period my lips shall remain sealed. Ladies, you know who you are, and you have my enduring gratitude and silence, which I trust you will reciprocate, especially the latter!

Throughout my twenties I carried on working, mostly in television but with occasional forays into live theatre. I know I was in a couple of episodes of *Z-Cars*, a gritty police soap set in fictional Newtown, somewhere near Liverpool. In those early days the studio shots went out live, interspersed with car chases in telecine. Unfortunately my Scouse accent wasn't all it might have been, somewhere between Birmingham and Cardiff someone said, and despite the best efforts of fellow actor Bill Kenwright I never quite managed to sound convincingly Liverpudlian, which may explain why I was never given a running part.

I did, though, appear in another long-running TV police soap opera, *Dixon of Dock Green*, a spin-off from a very popular film called *The Blue Lamp*, released in 1950. In the film, PC Dixon was killed, but by the miracle of television he rose from the dead five years later to become a regular feature of the BBC's weekend entertainment for some twenty years.

I appeared in only two episodes, and I think my role in the first was that of a motorcyclist, doubtless a badly-behaved one, and in the second, five years later, as a character called Len Kirby. I'm afraid my recollection of those instalments, the first made more than half a century ago, is not as clear as it might be. I do, though, recall that its star, Jack Warner, who was by then getting on in years, didn't dash around chasing people the way he did when, at the age of sixty, he first appeared on TV in the title role. I think by 1970 he was a sergeant. Perhaps it was a privilege of rank, but he spent most of his time standing still chatting to people.

CHAPTER SIX

ON BEING A REAL FILM STAR (FOR A FEW MONTHS)

Back in the 1960s the business of casting was a lot less formal than it is these days. I remember once being interviewed, along with several other young hopefuls, in the upstairs offices of Windward Films in Golden Square, in Soho, by the J Lee Thompson, director of such films as *The Guns of Navarone,* and *Where Eagles Dare.* At the conclusion of the interview we were asked to wait downstairs and to order whatever we wanted. They had their own bar on the premises! We interviewees spent about an hour or so down there, sampling the beer (it wasn't too bad, as I recall, despite being of the 'keg' variety) before the casting director came down.

Then it was, 'Okay, gents. See you in Austria.'

We were hired.

Some weeks later I was collected from my house in a chauffeur driven car, a Mercedes, I think. It was very big, very shiny and very, very ostentatious. I hoped the neighbours were watching and were duly impressed.

I was delivered to Heathrow, and in the VIP lounge (no less!) I met some of the people I was going to be working with – Larry Dann (of The Bill fame), George Innes (*The Italian Job* and

Elizabeth: The Golden Age) and John Hurt (of all sorts of fame) among them.

I had appeared with George Innes a year or two previously in an episode of London Weekend Television's *Blackmail* series called *The Taming of Trooper Tanner*, in which he played the title role. Once again I, as Trooper Harrington, found myself ending up dead. In a macabre twist it was my own real-life father who provided the coffin they carried me off in; he was by then head of scenery at LWT.

George and I found ourselves working together again in 1966, in an episode of ATV's, *Drama '66: Conduct to the Prejudice.* I was back in uniform, playing Private Strickland, one of the squaddies in a platoon commanded by Richard O'Sullivan, (Lieutenant Charles Reed), whom both George (Private Biggs) and I had occasion to salute and, to his amusement, address as 'Sir'. (We didn't really mean it, of course.)

Despite my having played soldiers before, the producers thought I needed to be re-trained in the art of square-bashing, which I should perhaps explain to the uninitiated was army shorthand for a lot of tedious marching up and down whilst wearing heavy hob-nail boots, carrying a rifle and being shouted at.

The man appointed to do the shouting was a retired regimental sergeant major, Norman Brittain MBE, reputed in his day to have had the loudest voice in the British Army. For some years he was an instructor at Sandhurst, the Army's school for would-be officers. It was his boast that whilst he had to call the cadets 'Sir' and they had to extend him the same courtesy, there was one great difference; *they really meant it!* Perhaps because in the twelve years since leaving the Army he had been an actor (appearing in several films, usually as a sergeant major) and a toast-master, his voice seemed to have lost none of its power as he strove to turn a gaggle of actors into something resembling (albeit somewhat vaguely) a professional fighting unit.

Drill can be demanding, confusing, tedious and painful all at once; as part of a team you had to put some effort into it for fear of unpleasant consequences for you and your comrades.   Drill instructors are supposed to put the fear of God into you, addressing you as 'You 'orrible little man,' (an RSM Brittain original, he claimed) and employing such threats as 'I'll 'ave you in chains in the Guard 'ouse!'

You had to struggle to make sense of and respond instantly to commands such as, 'Squad will move to the *Right* in threes, *Left* turn!' The last word was usually pronounced as 'Turn*ah*', which didn't help.

The command is correct, and there is a simple explanation of why that is so, but I will spare you that; as I said, drill can be tedious.

The painful part usually makes itself known after about half an hour of marching up and down in the 'Shoulder Arms' position. Those Lee Enfield Mark Four rifles are heavier than they look and carrying them can play havoc with your shoulder and back muscles. Factor in the earache from all that shouting and you'll begin to appreciate how some of us actors suffer for our art.

But I digress! Back to the story …

We eventually boarded a British European Airways flight to Munich; as we were flying first class more alcohol was consumed. I think the cabin crew, noting our youth and long hair assumed we were pop-stars and perhaps gave us even more of the fizzy stuff than we were entitled to. I thus only vaguely remember arriving in Munich, transferring to another black Mercedes – I think I had it to myself – and being driven to Salzburg, a journey of about 80 miles, arriving eventually at the very prestigious Hotel Bristol, where we each had our own suite.

We had arrived ahead of most of the rest of the company. They told us it was in order that we might 'acclimatise', by which I think what they really meant was 'sober up'. If they did, their ploy failed. With nothing to do for a week or two and plenty of money on hand to do it with we had a whale of a time exploring Salzburg and picking up a few trifles to take home –the odd Rolex and a few bespoke leather jackets.

One day though, tired of endless pavements and Mozartiana, we ventured out of town, ending up in the village of Anif, some fifteen miles from Salzburg. There we discovered the Hotel Friesacher, which was rather more to our taste than the Bristol. We inquired about the possibility of moving in, but the receptionist, observing our still over-long hair and slightly raucous dispositions, decided we were not the sort of guests they would welcome. However, once the word 'film' had been used to a slightly more senior member of staff, there was a miraculous change of heart; we sought and obtained the production company's blessing and arranged to move to the much less luxurious but considerably more relaxed surroundings of the Friesacher.

You may have gathered that this was a fairly major piece of work; I had in fact been selected to play a British soldier by the name of Alf in *Before Winter Comes*, a film starring David Niven and set in a displaced persons' camp in post-war Austria shortly after the end of the second World War. It may well have been the last big-budget no-expense-spared movie ever made. The film industry at the time seemed to be run by people who cared about their art and wanted to ensure their actors remained happy. How times have changed. Back then we had status and we were well-paid. We had stand-ins, chauffeur-driven cars and more money for everyday items (champagne, jewellery …) and other basic necessities than any sensible person could possibly need. Now it's all run by Harvard MBAs who can't really see the point of it all and certainly wouldn't want anyone to enjoy their work.

The movie was released in 1969, but the actual filming took place a year or two before that. It was to be my first and, regrettably, last experience of 'film-star treatment'. I really enjoyed it and if anyone wants to revive the old ways I'd be happy to help out in any way I can, but preferably with top billing. By way of compensation, though, I've enjoyed star-status throughout most of my TV career. It's similar, but with less champagne.

Our consumption of alcohol was at that time greater than today's experts would recommend as a sensible maximum, so it won't be surprising to hear that our standard of behaviour may on occasion have fallen below what would today, and perhaps even then, be considered acceptable. What can I say? Perhaps very little without incriminating either myself or my companions. Suffice it to say that security at the local zoo may have been less than total, and that on a certain evening, if two o'clock in the morning can be called 'evening', some unidentified people climbed over a fence and soon afterwards encountered a caged cat which they attempted to befriend. On discovering that the beast they were addressing as 'Pussy' was a much larger feline, a lion, in fact, they climbed back over the fence rather faster and a lot more sober than they had climbed in.

On location in Austria for *Before Winter Comes*

This all happened because a group of young actors found themselves in a foreign country with time and money to spend as they pleased. Each had acquired a taste for champagne. Fortunately everything changed when we were required to start actual work. Lines had to be learnt, scenes to be rehearsed and shot and even when we had lengthy periods of inactivity we had to restrain ourselves in order to be ready, and sober enough, to start again when required.

We were filming half-way up a mountain, where the set, in the form of a displaced persons' camp, had been built over a period of weeks prior to the arrival of the cast. There were also all the facilities you'd expect to find where people had to spend a lot of time hanging around. You could always find plenty to eat and drink and it was all of the best quality, though I seem to remember Chaim Topol's request for caviar being quietly ignored. He went on to play a character called Tevye both on the London stage and in the film version of *Fiddler on the Roof*, being chosen for the latter part in preference to Zero Mostel, who had played the role on Broadway. Could his expensive tastes explain his wonderfully heartfelt rendition of *If I were a rich man*?

By then I was getting used to having a chauffeur-driven Mercedes at my disposal (we each had our own) and fortunately there was a passable road up to the set; the title after all was *'Before' Winter Comes*.

Sometimes, David Niven invited me to accompany him on one of his afternoon walks and both his car and mine would follow at a respectful distance. I remember being slightly over-awed at first, but Mr Niven turned out to be friendly and charming, insisting from the start that we call him David. I had by then worked with many well-known and respected actors and directors, so could hardly have been 'star-struck', but even so, to find myself walking down an Austrian mountain with the best-known British actor in Hollywood still seemed like something rather special; perhaps the more so, as our two big black chauffeur-driven cars were identical!

My feelings of affection for David were shared by the whole cast, and we decided we should club together to provide him with a token of our appreciation. Accordingly a medal was commissioned, struck and duly presented to him. And yes, I believe it was of solid gold, unlike those cheap things they give to Olympic athletes. He wasn't expecting it; the director had told him that a re-take of one small scene was necessary and he had to walk from the 'orderly-room' out on to the 'parade ground' where we were all assembled, in uniform and carrying our rifles, loaded, but with blanks, ready for inspection.

David was not one to show unscripted emotion; when I approached him, bearing the medal on a cushion, he didn't turn a perfectly groomed hair. John Collin, who had played a character rejoicing in the name of Sergeant Woody, produced a scroll and read out a short message expressing the high regard in which we all held David. We then fired a volley of shots over his head, without, as far as I know, causing an avalanche.

David didn't show much emotion at the time but I later heard that he had treasured that medal and the scroll as mementos of a very happy time in his life. That evening he insisted on taking us all out for a meal, to a restaurant on the opposite side of a rather large, deep and very cold lake. It was a splendid meal and spirits were high. All went well until we were in the boat, about half way across the lake on the return journey, when Tony Selby (later to be seen in uniform again as Corporal Percy Marsh in the TV comedy series about National Service in the RAF, *Get Some In*) decided to jump overboard and swim the rest of the way. Fortunately we managed to rescue him.

Parties were frequent, but one of the more memorable was that hosted one Saturday night by the electricians, who seemed to outnumber the actors. They lived well away from us, in a villa rented for them by the production company. We had all heard it was to happen, but nobody was quite sure where it was to be held. It took place after work, so we all took our cars back to the production village, just as night was falling. No sign of a party, just silence and darkness. What we didn't know was that they had laid their hands on as many arc-lamps as they could, which was a lot, and suddenly the whole Tyrol region seemed to light up. The party was on.

CHAPTER SEVEN

HOME AGAIN

It was a year or two after my return from filming in Austria that I met Elaine, the young woman who was to become my first wife. We knew each other for barely a year before we married in September 1972, at Caxton Hall, no less; that was where everybody who was anybody did it in those days, and I was by then most definitely somebody. My best man was another actor, Hugh Janes, a former Conti boy who had a flat in the same block as mine. After the honeymoon my new wife and I moved to Telscombe Cliffs near Brighton.

Those first few months of marriage marked a busy period of my life, much of it spent on trains as most of my professional engagements happened in London and when I wasn't working or going to auditions and interviews in town I ran a small mobile disco catering for parties in the Brighton area. Despite having spent what was then a vast sum of money, the better part of £8,000, on a reasonably-sized house a few miles outside Brighton I was also able to afford a small boat and a large dog.

However, the marriage didn't work out and I suspect that between my first wife and Worthington, my Old English Sheepdog, the latter missed me more when I left to take up with another young lady. That's not to say that my wife, Worthington and I hadn't had some good times together, the three of us, and even now I regret giving up my boat, but I thought I would be happier with the sister-in-law of a fairly well-known folk singer.

I was wrong. That relationship didn't last either. I don't think it did much to enhance my reputation and wouldn't be surprised if a song about our affair and my less than gentlemanly behaviour were still being sung in the clubs and pubs of East Sussex.

Not long after Elaine and I separated I called round to see Hugh and bumped into the new tenant of my old flat. He was a young and decidedly gay dancer, who subsequently become Yul Brynner's dresser during the run of *The King and I.* On hearing the news that Elaine and I had decided to end our relationship, he wasn't surprised. 'These mixed marriages never work!' he said.

I met my second wife through one of my very rare forays into the world of amateur dramatics. Forbes Collins, an old friend of mine with numerous TV and film credits to his name, was teaching at the Mountview Theatre School, now the rather prestigious Mountview Academy of Theatre Arts (or so it says on its website!) which also had links with a local 'am-dram' society. They were putting on Tudor Gates' play, *Who saw him die?* an intense psychological drama about the struggle between a loveable but dangerous murderer and an apparently psychopathic detective. His leading man had dropped out, and Forbes was tearing his hair out trying to find someone to take on the role of 'loveable murderer' at short notice. Apparently I fitted the bill, and after much persuasion and, it must be said, quite a lot of beer, I agreed to help out.

Whilst doing so, I fell desperately in love with a fellow cast-member and as the feeling was mutual we decided to get married.

No Caxton Hall this time, just an ordinary register office on a rather dreary December day in Islington in 1978.

Once again Hugh Janes acted as my best man. Janet and I were very happy at first; indeed, because we couldn't bear the thought of a long enforced separation I even turned down the chance of a world tour of Hamlet with the Old Vic company, starting with a performance at Elsinore Castle in Denmark, a decision I regret even more than the loss of Worthington and my yacht.

That marriage unfortunately turned out to be no happier than my first. A friend of mine has a theory that actors should be forbidden from marrying until they are at least forty years old. Suffice it to say, then, that as a young man I was never very good at the marriage thing; only once I was safely into my forties did I risk another attempt at it, and then after a trial period lasting several years. I think I must finally have cracked it, though. Sally and I are still together and still happy after more than thirty years, and we have a son and two daughters; Elliot, Lucy and Polly.

But I'm getting a bit ahead of myself. This chapter's supposed to be about my twenties, which of course coincided with the Swinging Sixties, of which it has been said that if you can remember them then you weren't really there. I'm afraid my memory of them is a little hazy but I should stress that alcohol was probably the main culprit. For some reason the use of illegal mind-altering substances never appealed to me. On the other hand my sketchy memory could be down to some of the things I appeared in being inherently forgettable.

I was playing a character called Jacko Gregg in Crossroads, a soap opera about a midlands motel, for a while, but if you look at the full cast and crew list on IMDB you'll find I was in 'unknown episodes'.

Given that hundreds if not thousands of actors must have appeared in the series during its long run, the lack of detail is perhaps forgivable. At the time, though, being Jacko Gregg in *Crossroads* was something of a claim to fame, in a good way, the sort that gets you free drinks in pubs, but occasionally renders discrete assignations difficult; I shall say no more.

The full list on IMDb reads like a Who's Who of British acting talent over the three decades for which it ran. Even Bob Monkhouse got a look-in, playing himself for two episodes in 1966 – saves on make-up, I suppose.

I remember making a bit of a gaffe on my first day there. I sat in Noele Gordon's chair by mistake. As she was the star of the show, and had been since John Logie Baird first gave it air-time, this was no minor misdemeanour.

One of the things about film and TV sets (the sort actors work on, not the ones people watch) is that everyone, cast and crew alike, gets very possessive and territorial about their chairs. Invade their territory at your peril unless you are (a) very important, (b) very rich and therefore a source of funds for future ventures, and/or (c) incredibly famous. Being at that time none of the above I was given short shrift.

One of the more memorable Crossroads characters was Amy Turtle, played by Ann George. I say memorable and indeed she was, but her lines, apparently were not. Even she kept forgetting them, and that could be a problem in a live broadcast. Eventually they had to employ a special prompter and equip him with a button to mute all the microphones so that he could remind Ann of her line without the viewing public ever knowing.

One of the last things I did in that decade, back in 1969 in fact, was to play a character rejoicing in the name Hooray in a BBC Wednesday Play called *Sling Your Hook*. The plot was fairly simple; a group of Nottingham miners went on a coach-trip to Blackpool and drank a lot of beer. The way it turned out, a group of actors went on a coach trip to Blackpool and drank a lot of beer, the producers having been foolish enough to put the bottles intended for use in various scenes on the same coach as the cast.

We spent several evenings in Blackpool and some of the cast and I would go clubbing. One evening we found ourselves in a very pleasant club just off the promenade. There was a live band playing. Looking round the room I saw one particularly attractive girl and, being a polite and sophisticated young actor and perhaps under the impression that as such I was probably doing her a favour, went up to her and said, 'Excuse me, can I have this dance?'

Her response; 'Course you can! I don't want it.' must rank as one of the best put-downs in the long history of woman's cruelty to man. I shrank back into my seat. Soon afterwards I saw her dancing with someone else.

Her name was Norma. She was dancing with Warren Clark, but told him she'd rather be dancing with me. There being no objection from the girl I was dancing with, we swapped partners. Norma hadn't recognised either of us and when I told her we were in Blackpool to film a TV play she responded by claiming that she was the Queen of England. It was only once I'd persuaded her to come and see a night-shoot that she believed me. We were together for many months. I remember watching the first moon-landing with her in July 1969, and we continued seeing each other for quite a while after that.

It wasn't long after finishing *Sling Your Hook* that I went into *Crossroads*, which was of course filmed in Birmingham. The M6 was still unfinished in those days, which meant the drive to Blackpool at weekends was pretty arduous, and the drive back on a Monday morning even more so.

CHAPTER EIGHT
THE PROFESSIONAL DOLDRUMS

I turned 30 in 1974, nearly half way through that somewhat enigmatic decade which gave us (in no particular order) the three day week, Pol Pot, Richard M Nixon and Bernard Manning. The country was slowly coming down from the 1960s and what the public had seen as avant-garde and exciting just a couple of years previously now seemed distinctly passé.

I've already told you about my chequered career as a husband, but professionally the decade was something of a lean period. Somebody (it might have been my agent!) said I got married more often than I got acting jobs, and that's perhaps not too far from the truth. According to IMDb I only had about half a dozen engagements in the whole decade, none of them Earth-shattering. It started with a one-off performance in a series called *Conceptions of Murder*, about which I can probably remember even less than you, dear Reader. After that it all went a bit quiet.

A man has to eat, and doesn't need nearly as much rest as the profession seemed to be giving me at that time. Sometimes there was nothing for it but to do some actual work. Ever wondered where the staff of Grace Brothers learnt that air of fawning servility which so endeared them to a nation of telly-watchers? I strongly suspect that they, like me, took jobs in shops when times were hard. Moss Bros is a tailor's and dress-hire shop then based in Covent Garden catering for people posh enough to attend dressy events but not rich enough to buy their own clobber. Even today I believe a higher percentage of the staff are members of the actors' trade union, Equity, than than the Union of Shop, Distributive and Allied Workers (USDAW).

Back then, a whole gang of us, known at least to each other as the 'Fitters 500', whiled away the hours hoping either for a phone call from our agents or, failing that, the chance to earn a few extra shillings by persuading a customer to hire a non-black dinner jacket or to complete his costume with a colourful cummerbund. Grovelling and fawning were known to improve the chances of a decent tip. Occasionally someone famous and/or rich would turn up, usually because they were going to some once-in-a-lifetime event such as collecting a gong from Her Majesty or meeting Julian Fellowes for tea at the Ritz, but the regular staff made sure we were kept well away from such people, who coincidentally were usually the most generous where gratuities were concerned.

If all else failed, as it seemed to have done big-time back in the mid-seventies, there was always domestic work. Picture me in a pinny, feather duster in hand, practising my Ken Dodd impressions when I hoped nobody was looking.

I 'did' for quite a few well-known people, depressingly few of whom had heard of me, and including one very famous radio personality whose daughter went slightly nuts about me. It was the sort of work where you can discover quite a lot about your employer and I suspect I could have made a few grand from blackmail had I been so inclined, but I wasn't so I didn't. I don't sweep and tell, either.

Then there was casual work as a builder's labourer, which had the advantage of showing me useful skills I could later apply when 'doing it myself' on my own home. It also helped me to keep fairly fit and strong. Nowadays I have to pay to go to a gym to achieve the same result. By dint of much hard work back then I acquired, though I say it myself, a reasonably toned and fit body which perhaps compensated for my comparative poverty in attracting female company while I was between wives.

One of the more entertaining jobs I had towards the end of that period was as … well, I suppose I can say I was an entertainer. Not at the London Palladium or as a guest on *The Good Old Days*, I have to admit, but at least I was still in the business. Not to put too fine a point on it, I wore a coloured coat at a seaside holiday camp. I must have been fairly good at it because I was promoted to Entertainments Manager and given a camp of my own.

However, I'm getting ahead of myself. To begin at the beginning, my parents had booked a cruise and as I had nothing much else going on in my life at that time, professionally or romantically, they invited my then flat-mate and me to join them.

It was wonderful, and we both thoroughly enjoyed it, so much so that I began to see myself doing it full time. Not, obviously, as a passenger, even back in 1976 cruising was an expensive hobby, possibly even more so than today, but perhaps working my passage by appearing on stage, maybe telling a few jokes and the odd soliloquy here and there. Given plenty of time to spare for sitting in the sun supping something refreshing, it was a way of life I found very appealing.

Back on shore, I contacted the steamer company and asked if they had any vacancies. They didn't seem averse to the idea, but they said it might be better if I had some relevant experience; thus the blazer, the chalet and those oh-so-thrilling knobbly knees competitions. Well, that's how I think of it now, but the truth is that the 1950s had gone and the campers were starting to demand something a little more sophisticated. Fairground rides and comedians telling the sort of joke which these days would get them booed off the stage were what they wanted, and that's what they got. Please don't misunderstand me; I got on very well with the guests, perhaps, in some cases, rather too well, but I shall draw a veil over that.

Suffice to say that the second camp was a long way from where my soon-to-be second wife lived. In the end, though, it did little for my career. I didn't go to sea, and despite all that relevant experience I was never even offered a part in the BBC's very popular series, *Hi-De-Hi*. Though I shared a flat for a time with the camp comedian, the closest I got to *Hi-De-Hi* was my role in *Heidi*.

CHAPTER NINE

THE ROAD TO RECOVERY

Towards the end of the decade things started to pick up again. In 1978 I played Mr Gibbs in *Arsenic and Old Lace* and Mr Salt in a production of *The Gingerbread Man* at the Wyvern Theatre in Ipswich. That same year I played two parts, Cobweb the Fairy and the Master of Revels, at an Edinburgh Festival production of Shakespeare's *A Midsummer Night's Dream*. Our makeshift theatre was in reality the Church of Scotland Assembly Rooms so it was one of the very few times I have entered a religious building. If you've ever been to Edinburgh at festival time you'll know that accommodation is both scarce and expensive, but fortunately I was able to share a flat with another actor, Jeffrey Holland, the aforementioned camp comedian in *Hi-de -Hi!*

Our production of the Dream ran for about three weeks as far as I can remember, and went down very well with audiences. As usual, though, some nights were better than others. One of the best was when one of the other three fairies, played by an actor whose name I seem to have forgotten (for which he may well thank me!) had an unfortunate mishap with his headdress. To cut a long story short, it fell off, revealing his completely bald and make-up free head to the audience, eliciting one of the best laughs of the evening. I don't remember if anyone suggested that we keep it in.

Speaking of unfortunate hair incidents, it was shortly after my stint in Edinburgh that I was cast as Branwell Brontë in a Blue Peter Special Assignment called *The Brontës of Haworth*. My character famously had very red hair, and in the interests of accuracy the Beeb insisted on paying to have my hair dyed, possibly because they were keen to promote their colour television service, for which viewers paid a rather larger licence fee.

It was then that I discovered I was starting to show signs of male-pattern baldness. To my utter chagrin the Beeb noticed it too and decided that something had to be done. Accordingly I was fitted with a wig (very small, honestly!) which I somehow managed to keep in place despite the wind which whistled round Haworth throughout the week or so we spent filming there. I wondered what would have happened had that wig succeeded in escaping. Would a wardrobe person have rushed up to me with a replacement, uttering that traditional Blue Peter line, 'Here's one I made earlier?' Probably not ...

In 1979 I was offered the part of a Marxist polytechnic lecturer in the tour of Alan Ayckbourn's play *Ten Times Table*. Set in a ballroom, it involved the re-creation of a massacre. No easy task for a company of six. I won't give away too much more of the plot in case you're lucky enough to find a revival of it somewhere; I'd hate to spoil it for you, so suffice it to say that with a cast including Irene Handle (my some-time mother in *Heavens Above*) it was bound to do reasonably well. To say that we always played to packed houses would be a bit of an overstatement, though; I remember once seeing Irene peeping through the curtains just before the show started. Naturally I asked her what the house was like. 'Not many in today, dear,' she replied. 'Just a couple of lesbians and an Airedale ...'

Me as Eric with Dudley Long and Clare Clifford

Also in the cast were Phillip Bond, whom you might have seen in a TV Oz-spinoff called *The Wiz*, Jenny Tomasin who played a servant-girl called Ruby in the classic seventies series *Upstairs, Downstairs*, and Dudley Long.

Long by name and long by nature, at six and a half feet tall he was a walking beanpole who was great to be around on and off stage. Although his acting career never really took off, he had some success as a writer, and while we were on the tour he told me that he had submitted an idea to the BBC for a comedy series about a driving instructor. Aware that the Beeb was under a virtually constant bombardment of such ideas I thought little of it at the time, apart from wishing him well and planning a few consolation drinks for when the rejection-slip arrived.

I was wrong; Auntie liked it and wanted to make it. The consolation drinks turned into something of a congratulatory booze-up, in the course of which Dudley told me that he had written one part, that of Bert the Milkman, especially for me. Of course, these things take time and it was nearly three years before it all came together as *L for Lester*, starring Brian Murphy and Amanda Barrie, with John Forgeham, Linda Robson (with whom I would later work again in *Birds of a Feather*), Richard Vernon, Dudley himself as a half-witted policeman and, as promised, myself as Bert.

Me with Clare Clifford

We made six episodes which finally aired in 1982. People seemed to like it, and we all confidently expected to make a second series the following year, but it was not to be.

To this day I'm not sure what went wrong; not only did we fail to get a second series, we didn't even get repeated. Rumours abounded, of course; they always do. I will leave it to my readers to decide how likely it is that a programme which spent a fair amount of time taking the Micky out of policemen might have been thought unsuitable for times when real-life officers were involved in pitched battles against striking miners. If you want to see it, I'm told you should look on YouTube.

My next theatrical appearance was in 1980 in Richard Harris' splendidly funny play, *Outside Edge*. You may well have encountered it in one of its subsequent incarnations as a film and a very successful TV series, but the original was a simple stage play in which I played the part of Bob, an amiable alcoholic who was supposed to get steadily drunker as the evening progressed. Please suppress the urge to utter the words 'type-casting' and put out of your mind any suggestion that I might have had to imbibe in order to convince. Believe me, the last thing you should be when playing an inebriated person is genuinely under the influence, it simply doesn't work.

Acting is a skill, and alcohol impairs it. You might well convince your truly sozzled self that you are playing your part perfectly, but audiences are unlikely to agree. The rule was, no drinking before curtain up and no real alcohol on stage. Afterwards and off stage, though, was a completely different matter. I wondered at the time whether I could claim against tax for booze consumed in those circumstances as 'expenses incurred for research purposes'.

After starting life in at the Hampstead Theatre and the Queen's Theatre in 1979, Bill Kenwright's production toured the country successfully for several months. By the time I joined that tour, some of the original cast had moved on. I remember working with James Ellis, whom I knew from my Z-cars days, and Norman Rossington, said by some to have been in every film ever made, and it was in their company that I conducted a fair amount of the aforementioned research.

They eventually led me still further astray by introducing me to golf. That introduction did not, alas, lead to a second career and a place in the Ryder Cup team but the game has nevertheless given me many hours of pleasure and of course nearly as many hours of utter misery. Such is the nature of the beast.

James and Norman decided also to become the guardians of my moral welfare, ruining what had promised to be a rewarding romantic interlude by repeatedly banging on my hotel bedroom door, shouting loud and fairly lewd comments to each other in the corridor, ringing my room on the internal phone system (mobiles had yet to arrive in force) and posting silly notes under the door. Fortunately the lady concerned saw the funny side of it, as did I, albeit not immediately.

My character's stage wife in *Outside Edge* was played by a very attractive actress called Imogen Hassall. Tragically, Imogen, who had suffered the loss of a child followed by a divorce a few months previously, entered upon a long bout of depression culminating in her suicide later that year. After her untimely death she was replaced by an equally lovely actress, Deborah Brayshaw, whom some may remember playing a 'girl technician' in the 1972 *Doctor Who* story, *Day of the Daleks.*

Also amongst the cast was Liz Fraser, whom some of you may remember from her *Carry On* days. She proved to be quite at home in the theatre, too, but not quite as at home as her dog seemed to feel there. I think it must have been at the Oxford Playhouse, in March or April of 1980, that the animal, a Bassett hound as far as I can recall, managed to escape from her dressing room and make its way on to the stage, where it proceeded to relieve itself against the leg of a table before wandering off again to more enthusiastic applause than I remember ever receiving myself. It wasn't until many years later when I was on tour with Charlie Drake that I felt myself to have been so badly up-staged again.

I like television work but I have always preferred theatre, before a live audience, and best of all, on a West End stage. I was delighted, therefore, when late in 1980 my agent told me that a director called Alan Strachan wanted to see me about a possible part in Noel Coward's play *Present Laughter*. I duly travelled to Greenwich Theatre and auditioned for the part of Fred, valet to Garry Essendine, a matinee idol not quite in the first flush of youth. I don't recall what I used as an audition piece, perhaps he just had me read from the script. As often happens I was given no indication as to whether or not I had met with approval; it wasn't quite a case of 'Don't call us, we'll call you,' but close enough. I didn't call them, but I did pester my agent several times a week for a month or more, only to be told there was no news.

I had all but given up hope when she rang me to say that he'd heard from the Greenwich Theatre and they had indeed cast me as Fred. I learnt to my delight that I would be opening there at the end of January the following year. Of course, the rest of the cast was made up of a bunch of hopefuls, complete unknowns very unlikely ever to amount to much in the profession. They probably didn't. Have you ever heard of Donald Sinden? Dinah Sheridan? Julian Fellowes? Gwen Watford? Though, come to think of it … I had worked with Gwen once before when I was in *The Remarkable Mr Pennypacker* in Windsor many years earlier.

Me as Fred with Gwen Watford as Monica

Then there was the absolutely delightful Belinda Lang. I'd never shared a stage with her before, but had worked with her father, Jeremy Hawk (some time host of a game-show called *Criss-Cross Quiz* back when TV pictures had 405 lines and no colour) in *The Winslow Boy*. I had played the title role, though Jeremy had had more time on the stage than I did. That had been at the Queen's Theatre in Hornchurch, Essex. It gave me quite a bit to talk to Belinda about. It's always nice to share common ground with an attractive woman.

Me as Ronnie Winslow with Jeremy Hawk as Sir Robert Moreton

We had a lot of fun, on and off stage, during *Present Laughter*'s stays both in Greenwich and subsequently at the Vaudeville Theatre in London's Strand. We even managed to have a decent meal at the Houses of Parliament, thanks to the well-connected Julian (now Lord) Fellowes. We were definitely a hit, so much so that the BBC decided to record one of our performances for broadcast, for which a reasonably fat fee was forthcoming.

It was therefore a little bit worrying when we were asked one evening to remain on stage after our curtain call; such requests all-too-often preceded news that a run was coming to an end. It wasn't the case this time. Instead it turned out we were to be honoured by a visit from Her (now unfortunately late) Majesty Queen Elizabeth the Queen Mother who spent quite a long time chatting to members of the cast, shaking hands with each of us and telling us how much she had enjoyed the play.

Evidently my performance as the servant Fred had been fairly convincing, and I half wondered whether it might lead to a new career at the Palace. Her Majesty's visit meant that we didn't make last orders at the pub before setting off for home, but it was well worth the sacrifice if only for the mixture of pride, admiration and pure envy with which my mother greeted the news.

I did suffer one dent to my ego, though. I was at a cast-party in Donald Sinden's garden, sipping something refreshing, when Donald's wife Diana, walked past me with Belinda Lang. Noticing me, Diana asked Belinda whose driver I was. My sense of my own celebrity was only partially restored by the reply, 'That's Colin. He plays Donald's valet, Fred.'

'Oh yes! Marvellous actor,' replied Diana.

She was right of course! I was, and still am, a marvellous actor (though modest with it), but the damage was done.

After that, how could I ever have sufficient belief in myself to go voluntarily into some awful jungle and eat nothing but creepy-crawlies for no other reason than to be paid vast sums of money? On the other hand, maybe time is the great healer everyone claims it to be. Perhaps I have now overcome that trauma. If anyone reading this is in a position to help me find out, producers of *I'm a Celebrity* perhaps, please feel free to approach me.

Following the success of that first run of *Present Laughter* I was delighted when one evening some fifteen years later I received a phone call from Bill Kenwright asking if I fancied reprising the part of Fred in his new production at the Aldwych theatre.

I was in the local pub drinking with a mate (very unlike me, as those who know me will surely confirm) when the call came. It was noisy in the bar and it took a while to sort out the details, but it led to eight weeks at the Aldwych and eight more at Wyndham's Theatre in Charing Cross Road. Not bad when you realise it was a rush job. It was put on as a stop-gap when a musical called *The Fields of Ambrosia* closed early after only fourteen performances and disastrous reviews e.g. 'The show is clearly doomed but you would be a fool to miss it. It is one of the all-time great bad musicals,' from the Daily Telegraph.

Our sets were recycled from a 1993 production of *Present Laughter* at the Gielgud Theatre. Donald's role was taken by Peter Bowles. There was problem with those sets, though; they were held up *en route* by the police. There was a cordon around the area, some inconsiderate people having decided to blow up a bus in neighbouring Aldwych. Thankfully, those days seem to be behind us; Irish terrorism no longer threatens the West End Stage. Let us hope the same can soon be said of other such idiocies.

The show was directed by Richard Olivier, son of that famous actor who might have played a slime monster in *Doctor Who* if he hadn't been told it was only available because I had turned it down. However, I'm getting ahead of myself again. Back to the 1980s!

My dad had come on a long way since those early days of being a full-time lift mechanic and a part-time scenery shifter. I forget just when he started with Associated Rediffusion, but he worked his way up in the company and by the early 1980s, when the firm had morphed into London Weekend Television, was even in a position to take my mum away on a cruise.

I seem to remember they went on several such jaunts, but the one which was to change their and my life most dramatically was one to the Mediterranean. My dad's boss had an apartment near Marbella, and the two had arranged to meet up when the ship he and Mum were on called in at nearby Malaga, on the southern coast of Spain. My parents managed to find a taxi and eventually ended up at their friend's apartment, but the driver used the 'scenic route' so they managed to see a lot of the countryside on the way.

To cut a long story short they fell in love with the area. Back then there was a lot of open space, the present glut of hotels and holiday lets had yet to be built and you'd have been very (un?) lucky to find a fish-and-chip shop or a pint of Watney's Red Barrel.

Dad was also impressed by his friend's apartment. It was spacious, with air conditioning, decent bathrooms and quite near the beach. He would have been perfectly happy to rent or buy a similar one. My mother, though, had other ideas. An apartment would provide a very pleasant way to spend their holidays, but better still would be a villa. Not just any old villa, but one of their own design, built under their supervision and which could if necessary be enlarged and expanded should they so desire.

The idea grew on her during the course of the rest of the cruise, though I think my dad tried to put up a fight. My mother was, to put it mildly, a strong character and usually managed to get her own way.

By the time they returned to Blighty my dad had been persuaded to look into the possibilities. They started flying out to Spain to look for possible sites, but it was eventually another of my dad's friends who lived in the area who found what they wanted.

It was a largish plot with superb views of the Mediterranean, conveniently placed in the Las Chapas residential and beach urbanisation situated on the Costa del Sol, in the Malaga province of Andalucía. The main advantage of building on an urbanisation was that it would allow them to connect with essential services. The downside, though, was that lots of other things get built in the same area, spoiling your view and generally lowering the tone of the place.

However, the land was available, and at an almost affordable price, but Dad would have to act quickly, he was told, or it would be snapped up by property developers. My dad rang me and I was persuaded to help out, so that it became actually affordable.

It turned out eventually to be one of my better investments, but I have to say that back then it worried me. Nevertheless, and with the kind assistance of the Belgian friend who had found the land for them and in due course dealt with various solicitors and officials, the plot was purchased, an architect briefed, finance put in place, planning permission granted and work commenced on the building of the villa.

It took several years. The way it worked out there was that you paid so much for the foundations to be dug and the footings laid down, then work would stop until you paid for the next phase of construction, which might have been the exterior walls, then the interior walls and so on. My parents were ultimately very happy with the result, a comfortable modern villa with three good-sized bedrooms, ideal for family holidays. They decided to name it after the Christian Castilian knight Don Rodrigo Díaz de Vivar, also known as El Cid the eponymous hero of a 1961 film starring Charlton Heston and Sophia Loren. It was perhaps an odd name for a villa, you may think, but my dad's name was Sid.

My dad had some experience of planning and building villas by the sea. Some 50 years previously he had done the same thing near Warden Point on the Isle of Sheppey. If, that is, you're prepared to count a smallish beach hut with two rooms as a seaside villa. One of the rooms was a bedroom with a double bed and a couple of bunks, the other a small sitting room. In all it was about twenty feet by eight feet, built out of corrugated asbestos nailed to a timber frame, all put together by my dad with help from some of his friends. There were significant differences between what I then regarded as our house in the country and its modern Spanish counterpart, not least in the sanitary arrangements. I don't recall the first villa having any of those. There was a sink, but it wasn't connected to any sort of water supply. I suppose we must have had to fetch water in buckets from a stand-pipe, and I expect that would have been my job, though I can't remember doing it. I do remember that the beach wasn't up to much, and that there were the remains of a couple of Second World War torpedoes some other kids and I used to play on. I don't think they were still live, and I suspect that if they had gone off I'd have remembered, so I'm fairly sure they didn't.

My mother's initial satisfaction with El Cid didn't last for long. Shortly after the finishing touches had been put to the rather elegant wall surrounding the property she decided there was something lacking, namely a swimming pool. To be fair to her, they were a little way away from the sea, a two to three minute walk at least, and in any event conditions in the Med were not always ideal for a dip. Furthermore a pool in your own back garden was so much more convenient to sit by given the relative proximity of the fridge. A pool was, she said, essential, never mind that its construction would necessitate the partial demolition of the aforementioned wall. My dad wasn't very good at saying no to my mother so the project went ahead. It took a while and caused quite a lot of disruption but once completed it looked magnificent. However there was a problem. The soil in that part of Andalucía is very red due to the presence of iron in the clay. Given heavy enough rain that colour was transferred to the marble slabs surrounding our new swimming pool, spoiling its appearance and necessitating removal of the old pool, extensive digging out and replacement of the local clay with a non-ferrous variety, and rebuilding of the pool. Still it had to be done ... And in due course it was.

My parents spent a lot of their time in Spain, especially after my dad retired. For some reason they didn't do what most Brits in possession of a villa in Spain do, i.e. use it as a winter residence, but instead they went out there at the height of summer and returned to the UK in the colder, wetter and generally nastier months. I also spent as much time there as I could, and in later years I was able to take my wife Sally and our children out there as well.

Eventually my parents' health started to decline, and they decided to settle permanently in the UK. My dad offered to let me take over El Cid, but much as I loved the place I was not keen, not least because villa-owning is not a cheap hobby, what with local taxes, charges for water and so on. The area had also become a lot more built-up than it used to be, and the view from the Solarium, which used to be of open space stretching to the mountains in the distance, now featured lots and lots of buildings. The deciding factor for me was that properties like the villa had become targets for local criminals, and the Urbanisation's residents committee had decided the only course was to pay for armed guards to patrol the area. The villa was duly sold, and having been back to see it since I think we made the right decision.

Back to the 1980s. It was during the first run of *Present Laughter* that I met an actress called Jenny Hayes. Romance blossomed, and for a while we lived together, first in a village near Beaconsfield and later near the RFU's Twickenham Stadium, a move which brought Rugby to my attention. Alas my love for that sport has far outlasted Jenny's love for me. We split up amicably after a couple of years but even after more than three decades you will still see me wearing an England Rugby shirt on match days.

After the split I moved into a small flat next door to my then favourite pub, the Duke of Cambridge just a few yards down the road. I spent a lot of time there and was instrumental in converting some of the other regulars, mostly from the pub's remarkably unsuccessful darts team, to the game of golf, and was proud to become the first President of the Kneller Golfing Society. I may still be the president because nobody's ever told me I've been deposed or replaced. On the other hand, I haven't paid any dues either so I can't blame them if my reign has come to an end.

It was while I was living there that I met my present wife, Sally, at a social event for divorced and separated people held in a pub I'd never visited before. I'd heard about these events from regulars at the Cambridge, and went along without really knowing what to expect. My mates and I spent most of the evening sitting as a little group, and although I had noticed Sally from a distance it wasn't until they announced that the next dance was to be the last that I plucked up the courage to go and speak to her.

We danced, and afterwards I asked her for her phone number. As she claimed not to have one that could have been the end of everything, but fortunately I had the good sense to promise to see her next time, and the even better sense to keep that promise. Our relationship grew over a period of several weeks, during which time she admitted she did have a phone number, and gave it to me. Eventually I left my flat near the Cambridge and moved in with her and Lucy, her daughter from a previous relationship, whom we subsequently adopted.

It wasn't long before Sally told me she was expecting another child. Our daughter Polly was born in the autumn of 1987, and her brother Elliot came along less than two years later. Knowing that I'd tried it twice and failed miserably both times Sally and I were both a little reluctant to risk tying the proverbial knot, but in 1990 we went ahead and did it anyway, at a very low-key ceremony in the local register office. The best thing about it was that Polly, our three-year-old daughter, was a bridesmaid.

I think I must somehow have managed to grow up a bit by then because we're still together after getting on for thirty years and we now have three grown-up children and two grandchildren, all of whom we love dearly.

Tragically, though, our first grandson, Oliver, was born with health problems which were eventually and after much pain and suffering to take him from us when he was just nine years old. His parents, Lucy and her partner Robert, have struggled hard to come to terms with it all, yet somehow they and their two other children, Anna and Fred, have managed to weather that storm.

CHAPTER TEN

WHO'D HAVE THOUGHT IT?

I mentioned earlier that I was at school with a boy called Graeme Harper, and that we have remained friends ever since. You should not assume, though, that he was always in a position to put work my way. When in about September of 1984 he told me that he was going to be working on a children's drama series called *Doctor Who* it was more in hope than in expectation that I asked him if there was a part in it for me. I felt no anger or resentment when he told me there wasn't, although I will admit to being a little bit disappointed.

We were in the BBC club at the time, a wonderfully relaxing bar in the sorely-missed TV Centre in Wood Lane, between White City and Shepherd's Bush. If you sat there long enough – and I always tried to make sure that I did – you would see everybody who was anybody in the world of television. The building is still there but they've turned it into a block of flats, sorry, 'luxury apartments'. Such a shame; it was where I spent much of my time in the 1960s and I have some very fond memories of the place. Never mind: it doesn't do to get maudlin about these things and I'm digressing again.

I think it was a few weeks later that my agent rang me to say Graeme had changed his mind and that there might after all be a part for me in *Doctor Who*.

I was to play a mutant of some sort, and would be filmed emerging from a lake of that slime the BBC used to manufacture by the gallon, almost exclusively for use in *Doctor Who*. I think Noel Edmonds also tapped into the supply later for his *House Party* game-show in the 1990s.

Needless to say I was very excited at the prospect. Please don't tell Graeme, but I spent hours working out how best to play my part, contemplating my motivation and even investing in fifty gallons of what I hoped was slime similar to the Beeb's in order to practise my emerging techniques. As a matter of fact, that simply isn't true, but had I done all that, I would have been wasting my time.

When I went along to White City to read for the part I found myself sitting in a room with Graeme, his casting director and John Nathan-Turner, aka JN-T, who had produced the series from its inception. I duly read for the part of the Mutant. It wasn't all that challenging, I think I just had to slurp a lot. But then Graeme said he would like me also to read the part of a humanoid called Lilt.

A few weeks later I received a phone call from my agent saying I was being offered the part of Lilt. Having nothing better to do at the time, I gratefully accepted.

Doctor Who fans will know that my character was one half of a double act; the other half, Takis, was played by my old friend Trevor Cooper. Graeme apparently saw us as a sort of extra-terrestrial Laurel and Hardy. In those days actors were allowed plenty of rehearsal time, and for a couple of weeks I commuted from my home near Twickenham to the BBC's rehearsal-rooms just north of the A40 (another sorely-missed facility long-since sold off).

Before the rehearsal-rooms opened, rehearsals would be held in all sorts of places; village halls, disused warehouses, schools or any convenient space that could be hired reasonably cheaply. So the Acton Hilton, as it came to be known, marked a vast improvement.

There were about six floors, each with two large rehearsal spaces. On the top floor there was a cafeteria adjudged by many to be second only to the BBC TV Centre's club when it came to meeting people.

I'd never been much of a science-fiction fan, but those two episodes of *Revelation of the Daleks* were fun to make. The Doctor at the time was Colin Baker, and his companion, Peri, was played by Nicola Bryant. It was a star-studded cast; Terry Molloy (whom some of you will know from his years playing Mike Tucker in BBC Radio 4's *The Archers*) played the evil arch-Dalek, Davros, Alexei Sayle played a DJ, and Eleanor Bron, Clive Swift, and Jenny Tomasin were all in it.

Somewhat surprisingly, Lord Olivier wasn't. Rumour had it that the great man was a Doctor Who fan, and might have been persuaded to accept a cameo role. The story goes that Graeme rang Lord Olivier's agent, but it seems that the call came to an abrupt end when he mentioned that the part of slime-covered mutant was only available because I had turned it down ... I hadn't of course; Graeme had simply decided I would make a good Lilt. The part of slime-mutant eventually went to actor and stunt-man Ken Barker.

At the time I had no idea how important a part *Doctor Who* was going to play in my life. It was just a job in a children's TV series, and although it had been going for a few years it had nothing like the sort if cult following it enjoys these days. Appearing in the show for the second time some twenty years later brought home to me just how much the business had changed in that time, and how much damage the bean-counters had done. Let me explain ...

When we recorded *Revelation of the Daleks* we actors were encouraged to do our jobs properly, so before we went anywhere near the studio at Television Centre we all knew not just our own lines but those of the other people in our scenes. That enabled us to think about how we should say our words and how we would react to what was happening around us; not just in the way we said our lines, but our facial expressions and movements.

Here's how it was all managed: the first thing to happen was the filming of exterior shots. In *Revelation* it all happened on the planet Necros, on which the Doctor and Peri arrived to find themselves in a snow-covered landscape, complete with a corpse-infested swamp. It was all done on film. In fact I think it was the last time actual film was used on *Doctor Who*'s outdoor shots; all future such scenes were shot straight on to video tape, the format which had until then been used exclusively for indoor shots. I can only assume someone had invented a waterproof TV camera. However, I digress. Suffice it to say that more or less everything which happened in the first half of the episode had already been put (literally) 'in the can' by the time indoor rehearsals started.

That happened on a Monday morning, and I can still remember the occasion well. It started as a sort of coffee morning, hosted by Graeme, where we all sat round a table and told the others who we were and what or whom we were playing. That was the prelude to a first read-through; no acting required, just a simple saying the words out loud. Someone with a stop-watch timed us so that Graeme and the rest of the team could get a rough idea of how long to allow for each scene. If you've been paying attention you will recall that over-running was not an option for drama productions, especially if they were to be followed immediately by a news broadcast. The writer would be present at this read-through in order that any mistakes could be picked up and corrected, and 'pink pages' i.e. a corrected version of the script, issued to the cast. They were probably printed on pink paper so that the actors wouldn't muddle the two versions and produce even worse mayhem.

During that round-the-table read-though members of the crew busied themselves on the floor of the rehearsal studio improvising sets for us to work on later in the day. Lines of coloured sticky-tape marked where there would be walls, doors and so forth when we came to the actual performance. In readiness for the process of 'blocking' that afternoon, the crew also put in place any solid items, chairs, tables, kitchen sinks or whatever-which would be part of the real set, and around which we would in due course have to move.

Blocking was not, as its name might suggest, something we did in order that we could be sure of getting in each other's way; quite the opposite, in fact. It enabled us to plan how we would move around the set as each scene unfolded and gave Graeme an idea of where he should place the cameras (back then they used a multi camera setup; not so now) and how they should move in relation to the action. All parties involved would make notes in the hope of avoiding muddles and mix-ups later on. Never 100% successful in that respect it was better than nothing, and it's a technique they still use in theatre.

We'd go through it all again at least once before lunch, then again in the afternoon and several times the following day. By Wednesday we were expected to know our lines, and be able to add a bit of depth to our performances. We could experiment, exchange ideas and make suggestions. As I think I may have said before, Graeme is the kind of director who will let you do that and might even take your suggestions on board.

The process continued on the following day, so that by Friday we were ready for the technical run-through. That's when the sound and lighting people came in to see what they would have to do and the logistics of making sure that the right props were going to be to hand when required were sorted out. The make-up artists and cameramen would be there to watch a run-through or several, and identify and hopefully resolve any problems, so that come Saturday, when we moved into our studio at Television Centre, after only a few more rehearsals, with cameras, the cast and crew would function as a well-oiled machine to produce a flawless performance fit for editing and subsequent broadcast.

As Mr Crane

As Mr Crane with Cybermen

Twenty years or so later that had all changed. We shot the two-parter in Wales. In *Rise of the Cybermen* and *Age of Steel*, I played the evil villain Lumix's only slightly less evil henchman, Mr Crane. There was very little time for rehearsal. Having been in possession of my script for quite a long time beforehand I knew my lines and had a reasonably clear idea of how I was going to say them, trusting to luck that it would gel tolerably well with how my colleagues said *their* lines.

We shot each scene after only the briefest of read-throughs. There was no scope for discussion with other members of the cast, no exchange of ideas, just the expectation that we would get on with doing a professional job of work as quickly (and therefore as cheaply) as possible. There was very little time to see how the other actors were going to react. It might be argued that this lent an air of spontaneity to the performance, eliminating that stilted earnestness which some say marred performances in previous decades. For my part I can only say that this new approach left me feeling a bit like a Cyberman myself.

CHAPTER ELEVEN
AFTER WHO ...

It was a year or so after my first appearance in Doctor Who that I joined the cast of a TV series, *The Collectors*, about our ever-popular Customs and Excise service (now Her Majesty's Revenue and Customs). I was to play a lorry-driver suspected of bringing more into the country than was shown on his paperwork. I got the part largely because I could drive a lorry; in fact, I had a full Heavy Goods Vehicle licence, one of the many skills I had picked up over the years.

Anyone wishing to become an actor should learn to do other jobs as well; one of the very few advantages of the 'lean' periods in an acting career is that opportunities to acquire new skills and observe all manner of different people tend to arise while you're doing other sorts of work in order to feed yourself and your family and keep a roof over your heads.

Among other things, I am quite handy with electric irons, vacuum cleaners and other household equipment; I can do a bit of brick-laying and general building work and serve customers in up-market clothes shops. Thanks to those military training films I mentioned earlier I also know my way round a frogman's suit and I can blow things up. I have also done a few non-military training films. I did one for Marks and Spencer, which was shown to all new recruits. I think I played a warehouse manager. Sally teased me about it for quite a long time. It was during one of my lean periods, and she had taken a Saturday job to help make ends meet. You can imagine the reaction when, on being shown the training film in the company of thirty other new recruits, she announced rather too loudly, 'That's my husband!'

My obtaining a licence to drive lorries came about because during a rather protracted lean period I was offered the chance of driving a pantechnicon full of scenery from place to place for a major television company. OK, I confess, there was an element of nepotism at work; it was the TV company my dad worked for.

In order that I might do so they very generously offered to pay for me to attend a one-week intensive driving course, after which I would take my HGV test. Being somewhat skint at the time I jumped at the opportunity, and somehow managed to pass first time.

As it happened, I didn't have to work as a lorry driver for very long. Something else turned up so that instead of having to transport scenery I was able to concentrate on not bumping into it, but the HGV licence landed me one or two good parts.

Playing a character called Dave Chapman in *The Collectors* was interesting if for no other reason than that I found myself working with an actor called John Bindon. He was known to have gangland connections and was rumoured to have spent some time on the island of Mustique in company, he claimed, with Princess Margaret, though she later denied that they had ever met, let alone had an affair. Despite all that and his hard-man reputation, I found him perfectly affable and professionally competent, which was just as well for he was still thought not to be the sort of man you wanted as an enemy.

Another word or two of advice to young and/or would-be actors: do *not* claim you can do things if you can't. Saying things like, 'Of course I can ride a horse / fly a helicopter / swim the English Channel with one hand tied behind my back,' might (but probably wouldn't) impress a casting director, but can also come back to bite you. At the very least and if you're lucky you will end up feeling very embarrassed. More serious possible consequences I will leave to your imagination.

The slump I mentioned earlier seemed very bad at the time, but it didn't last forever, and most years between 1980 and today have seen me involved in at least one major TV production, some memorable, others perhaps forgotten by most people.

I've had a few spells in hospital, mostly in Holby City. I learnt to drive a Tube train in 1991, when I appeared in *London's Burning*. I had hoped to get a chance to drive a 'proper' train in 1996 when I worked with Jasper Carrott and Robert Powell in an episode of their popular series *The Detectives*. Disappointingly, however, I found I was playing the guard.

Other characters I have played have driven ambulances (*Boon*, 1990), taxis (*Birds of a Feather* 1991), milk floats (*L for Lester* 1982) and I can't remember what else in various plays and TV series. I played a Roman soldier, a centurion, no less (in the officer class at last!) in *The Brittas Empire* (1994), I had parts in *Minder* (1993), *Shine on Harvey Moon* (1995), a couple of appearances in *Doctor Who* ... I could go on, but it would probably be easier if you looked me up on the internet.

Some things do stand out, though not necessarily for the right reasons. In 1995 I landed a part in *Cynthia Payne's House of Cyn*, a docudrama about Cynthia Payne in which I played the suitably anonymous Client #2. It was shot at the former brothel in Streatham, and involved a fair amount of nudity, though I didn't actually do a full frontal; the closest I got to that was wearing a French maid's costume, until bed-time, that is, when most of it came off and several young ladies joined me under the covers … I'm an artist and I can control my urges. Put aside those smutty thoughts.

Cynthia herself was present throughout, as were several of her former employees, though they were played by younger women when shooting started. We all had a guided tour of the house, including one particular torture chamber which we were assured had been the favourite room of a certain late prime minister's husband. I shall refrain from naming him to spare the family's blushes. It was in many ways (though perhaps not in the first way that might spring to mind) great fun to do. I still treasure the Luncheon Voucher Cynthia presented me as a souvenir. Famously, clients paid individual sex-workers in Luncheon Vouchers, which they could exchange for sandwiches in local cafés or for cash from Cynthia at the end of the week.

I don't think the programme was ever aired on live TV but embarrassingly it was released on video-cassette where the quality wasn't brilliant. I say embarrassingly because copies of the tape turned up on a bric-a-brac stall at my daughter's school fête.

Our production was subsequently eclipsed by the major film *Personal Services*, released a couple of years later. It became available on YouTube, but that account was 'terminated due to multiple third-party notifications of copyright infringement.'

Some of my work has been eminently forgettable, and some has been memorable for the wrong reasons, such as the character's name. In 1995 I was Florist Gump, a pub-customer in an episode of *Nelson's Column* which I think might have been about a journalist.

I played a shop-keeper in *Maisie Raine,* working again with Pauline Quirke, and even had a small part in *East Enders.*

Me as Chas with Kevin Whateley

One of the highlights of that era, though, was playing Chas, the landlord of the local pub, in the last-ever episode of the detective series *Morse,* based on the eponymous hero of Colin Dexter's novels. Entitled *The Remorseful Day,* mine was the episode in which John Thaw collapsed on a college lawn and subsequently died in hospital. My main scene was with Morse's long-suffering sidekick, Detective Sergeant Lewis, played by Kevin Whately and subsequently promoted and given a side-kick of his own, Detective Sergeant Hathaway played by Laurence Fox.

My scene with Kevin was quite long, and I'm fairly sure that what I was able to tell him proved to be the key to solving the whole mystery. Or maybe it was just about getting the right sort of beer for his boss. It still seems to come round on TV quite often. I must remember to watch it again.

Sadly, John Thaw was to die for real about two years after we made that episode; perhaps he knew when we were shooting that he had cancer, but if he did then he didn't let it show. He was on good form at the wrap party which was held not in Oxford but in the Water and Steam Museum near Kew Bridge in west London, and was, as far as I can remember, a good party.

In the early part of the current millennium, 2001, I think, I was offered a part in a series called *Down to Earth,* which at that time starred Pauline Quirke and the late and greatly missed Warren Clarke, both of whom I had worked with before. You may also recall that Warren and I spent a memorable evening in Blackpool. He was the one who first danced with Norma … but that was an amazingly long time ago. Pauline, who played Warren's screen-wife in *Down To Earth,* was an old friend from *Birds of a Feather* and *Maisie Raine.*

Their characters were based on the series' creator, Faith Addis, and her husband. The story was that they had sold their home and business in London and bought a farm somewhere to the west of Bristol. I was initially offered just one episode, playing a rather grumpy individual called Bob Bailey. It all went well but I moved on and did other things; a TV mini-series called *'Orrible,* an episode of *Judge John Deed* and a film called *Redemption Road* which as far as I know, never went on general release but is probably available to view somewhere out there in cyberspace if you look hard enough. I'm afraid I haven't been able to find it, nor any mention of it. If you decide to look, don't be taken in by the US movie of the same name released in 2010.

It was at some time in late 2002 or early 2003 that the BBC asked me in to discuss a project which I rather liked the sound of. It was a one-off crime-series called *The Murder Game*, and was in many ways an actor's dream as you had complete control over your lines, responding to questions from a coach-load of amateur sleuths, all of whom had received some brief training in the art of detection and crime-solving from some friendly police persons.

On their way back from their training, which had happened somewhere in Yorkshire, I believe, so they must have taken a very strange route, they drove through a little village in Kent, where they saw ambulances, police, flashing blue lights and people milling around aimlessly wondering what they should do next about a certain dead body.

Aha! Coachload of freshly-trained homicide detectives to the rescue!

Over the course of a mere seven episodes they worked out who did it and why. Fairly run-of-the-mill stuff, but very appealing to the actors because of the huge amount of research they had to put into knowing their characters.

The 'players' (for want of a better word I will describe them as such for it was, I suppose, a sort of game-show) were free to approach any of the people in the village and ask them whatever they liked, relevant or irrelevant. The actors taking part had thus to know all about their screen-selves from birth date down to inside leg measurement, education, employment, family, you name it. The actor had to know it in order to be able to give convincing and consistent answers to all questions asked.

It would not do to tell one player that you were born in, say, Stogumber and another that you took your first breath in Bishops Lydiard. Woe-betide you, too, if you couldn't give the names and dates of birth of your kids.

The BBC had adopted the idea from an apparently successful show in the USA – I have little doubt that they spent oodles of licence-fee money on it – but it took quite a lot of setting up, and by the time they were almost ready to go I had been asked to reprise my role as the grumpy Bob Bailey in *Down to Earth,* on the tacit understanding that he would go on to be quite a major character as the love-interest for Warren's mother in law. The show had been going for some time and was very popular, so it sounded like a good career move.

Alas, writers are fickle beasts. They no sooner settle on one plot-line than they decide to change it. Suddenly Warren's ma-in-law lost interest in me (though I have no idea why!) and my part seemed to be getting smaller, something which they tell me is not uncommon for older actors. The writing seemed to be on the wall; there were rumours that Pauline and Warren were on the verge of moving on and there was to be some re-casting. Such rumours tend to fly around the sets of most long-running series and can usually be discounted, but I seem to remember that in the second episode I did in the 2003 season Angela Griffin joined the cast as potentially the new owner of the farm, and Pauline and Warren did indeed move on at the end of that run.

Their characters were based on the series' creator, Faith Addis's life. Although Bob Bailey might have been kept on under the new regime, his would no longer be a major part, and because *The Murder Game,* which suddenly seemed a much more attractive proposition and probably a good career-move, was due to start production I (through my agent) asked the BBC to release me from my contract for *Down To Earth* and allow me to do that instead.

It was pointed out that whilst I featured quite prominently in the two episodes I had already done my character was barely noticeable in the script for the third episode, the one in which I was supposed to be involved in some fairly heavy scenes with the lady in question, though it went out before the 'watershed' so they couldn't have been too steamy. This, we argued, was so far from what I had been led to expect as to render me dispensable for that third episode.

I had by then been offered a part in *The Murder Game,* and whilst they hummed and hawed for a bit they eventually gave in, and I set off for Kent to become Frank Prior. I say I set off for Kent, but a lot of the work was done during several weeks of rehearsal in London. We went through every possible scenario, asking each other the questions we expected the 'detectives' would ask us, not just, 'Where were you at the time of the murder?' or 'Do you own a gun?' but 'Did you grow up in this village?' and 'What schools did you go to? Did your daughter go to the same school? Did she do well? How many GCSE's did she get?' and so on and so forth, until our legends were really ingrained in us. There was no script; it was all improvisation. I think it must have been a bit like the training they give to spies and undercover police officers.

Mine was a tough part to play. The victim was my character's daughter, and she had been foully done in on the eve of her wedding. I won't say too much more about the plot, just in case you have a chance to see the whole thing; I wouldn't want to spoil it for you.

As I had expected, it was both challenging and very good fun; I was for a time a prime suspect, I think, but then so was just about everybody else. We all had high hopes of another series. Implausible, perhaps, that there could be more than one murder in the same village, but just look at *Midsomer Murders*.

Unfortunately the series received less than rave reviews. Audiences, initially quite high, dwindled over the seven weeks or so until at one point both viewers got up to make a cup of tea at the same time. It was not a success, and some fifteen years on there has been no attempt to make another one.

Although I'm still available, I don't get anything like as much acting work as I would like. The upside of that is that I am able to attend a lot more conventions. I think it was Frazer Hines who first suggested some fifteen or twenty years ago that I should start going to them as they were both fun and potentially financially rewarding. At the very least you would get your expenses paid, accommodation and travel, and they happened all over the world (with the possible exception of Antarctica).

He made it sound very exciting, and I was definitely interested, but I was haunted by the vision of my turning up at some swish venue, clutching photos and felt-tip pens ready to offer signed pictures to my public only to be asked 'Colin who?' After all, *Doctor Who* had been running on and off for more than forty years, and my total on-screen time was probably less than a single hour; why should anyone remember me?

I put that question to a very charming man with a broad Glasgow accent who rang me one day, perhaps out of the blue or perhaps after some judicious prompting from Frazer, to ask if I would consider attending a Doctor Who convention in his home town. I was flattered. I asked him if anybody would know who I was. His reaction was one of astonishment. He had absolutely no doubt that I would be both remembered and recognised, not to mention made very welcome by the many fans of the show who would be attending. His exact words were, as far as I can recall, 'I can assure you, Mr Spaull, they will know exactly who you are.' He was right; much to my surprise they did.

The deal was, as Frazer had suggested, that my expenses would be paid and I could keep any money I might make from selling autographed photos of myself. It sounded almost too good to be true, and although I agreed to go my nagging doubts persisted. Luckily one of my friends knew someone who was a long-standing *Doctor Who* fan and had attended many conventions. That friend, a barrister called Andrew, agreed to meet us both for drinks in Richmond. He turned out not just to remember me but to know even more about my appearances in *Doctor Who* and other things than I knew myself.

It seems that having been in both the ancient and modern versions of *Doctor Who* made me something of a rarity, and thus a much more desirable convention guest. I would, he assured me, be warmly welcomed wherever I went.

He was right. The fans who attend conventions are a marvellous bunch and I've never had a bad experience. Well, almost never.

Beware of the Glasgow Doctor Who Appreciation Society (GDWAS). Their spies are everywhere and they keep close tabs on people associated with the programme. I know this because when I was working for a company called Tern Television, narrating their *Spa of Embarrassing Illnesses* series, I used to travel to Glasgow about once a week to speak lines such as, 'There's mud, sweat, tears and twice-daily colonic irrigation,' in what I hoped would pass for a vaguely 'northern' accent. The GDWAS found out, I know not how, and after each session at Tern's Union Street studios persons acting on their behalf would waylay me, drag me off to some pub or other and force me to drink copious amounts of beer. Terrible people!

Luckily for them (and me!) I quite like beer and have been a member of CAMRA, the Campaign for Real Ale, for some years now. Pubs are, in my view, amongst the most civilised places on the planet. Wherever you go you can usually find a hostelry where they will make you feel welcome, and where you can drink proper beer, made with yeasts that work at temperatures above freezing point and which actually impart some flavour to the brew.

The trouble with lager is that it's made using yeast that works at low temperatures, and as there are very few strains of such yeast most products end up tasting much the same as the rest, or would do if they weren't served so cold that you can't really taste anything anyway.

So far my liver has managed (touch wood!) to resist the onslaught of the considerable quantities of beer I have sent it for processing over the years. It even tolerates wine. I have relatively recently abandoned claret for Chablis in that department, but the liver doesn't seem to mind. I will drink spirits, but only if there is no viable alternative.

The best pubs are the ones where you don't need ear-plugs; unfortunately these are becoming relatively rare. I can understand playing a little carefully-chosen background music if a pub is nearly empty and the silence might be intimidating, but why oh why do they have to turn it up when more people arrive? It just makes people start having to shout to each other to make themselves heard. The bar-staff find the shouting is drowning out the music and so they turn it up, which makes people have to shout louder, which … well, you can see where that's leading,

I'm sure, if like me you go to the pub with friends to enjoy a drink and a chat, both elements are important, so when the music drowns out the conversation half the pleasure vanishes. Factor in fruit machines and mobile phones and you are half way to persuading me to buy my beer in the supermarket and drink it at home. As far as I can remember, though, the pub the GDWAS dragged me to was reasonably civilised so that experience didn't put me off going to conventions. Or, indeed, doing voice-overs, of which more anon. First, a little more about conventions.

If you're one of those people who has been to every *Doctor Who* event ever held anywhere in the world (and I'm sure that must apply to at least a few of you) then you should skip this section because your memory's probably better than mine and you'll find my many mistakes irritating.

One of the first conventions I attended was held at Riverside Studios in Chiswick, not far from Hammersmith Bridge. It's a place I used to know fairly well, and which is familiar to any *Doctor Who* fan as the place where early episodes were made in the 1960s. William Hartnell changed into Patrick Troughton back in 1966, nearly twenty years before my first appearance in the programme. As with certain other ex-Beeb centres Riverside is currently being re-developed (along with its neighbour, the former Queen's Wharf building) to include about 165 flats as well as, apparently, some studio facilities, a restaurant and a café-bar. I quite liked it when it was scruffy and we did *Dixon of Dock Green* with wobbly scenery (though not as wobbly as the *Crossroads* scenery). Never mind. The convention was good fun and helped me prepare for the many which were to follow. My old friend Trevor Cooper – Takis to my Lilt in *Revelation of the Daleks* – was there and I've been bumping into him at Docfests (as some people insist on calling conventions) ever since.

Generally speaking, convention organisers treat their guests very well. If we're lucky, we get the full-on five-star treatment we obviously deserve. Sometimes we don't; no names, no pack-drill, but ...

However, whenever I feel badly done-by I just think back to the bad old days of theatrical digs, some of which had had a bathroom added to the back of the house because it was originally built without one. I remember one particular digs where you gained access to the bathroom via the kitchen. Coming back to the digs one evening after an after-show meal I was on my way to avail myself of the facilities when the landlady informed me of the rule, 'No solids after ten o'clock.' My reply, dear reader, I shall leave to your imagination.

Convention accommodation is generally much better; we get fed and watered (though 'wined and dined' might be a better description) and are usually assigned an assistant to deal with any problems we might encounter and deal with the sordid business of taking the money for all the photos and autographs we sell at the event. I say 'all' and it has to be said that for the most part we do pretty well out of those sales. Some convention organisers let us provide our own photos and pocket the takings, others will provide us with photos and expect us to sign them for all comers in return for a flat fee. That, of course, can work to the guest's advantage if a convention is poorly attended, as some are. Even with a moderate attendance it saves a lot of hassle over getting your own photos printed and lugging them around on trains, planes and automobiles – and, of course, ships, of which more anon.

At a well-attended convention, though, you can end up with tired wrists and empty pens for no appreciable extra reward. The upside seems to be that organisers make money from conventions, and the 'convention industry' seems to be growing, which means I get more and more opportunities to enjoy the company of the fans and the joys of airport lounges whilst making a few very welcome shillings, dollars or Euros.

Simply sitting at a desk with a pen and a cheerful smile is all very well, but sometimes we are allowed up from our tables to do more interesting things. Often I have been asked to be part of a panel, when together with some of my fellow guests I am led to the front of some sort of small theatre or lecture hall and told to speak a little about myself and then to answer questions from the audience. There is usually a moderator who protects me from the more awkward questions, but the subject matter is by no means limited to *Doctor Who* trivia, and some of them probe areas of my life I have either forgotten or would wish to forget.

Graeme Harper and I have been on several panels together and are generally reckoned to be a good double-act, or so I'm told. However, I will be the first to admit that I am no expert on the good Doctor's adventures and exploits. I was, and remain, a jobbing actor. Furthermore, a good few years have passed since I played Mr Crane and even more since I was Lilt. My store of Who-related anecdotes is therefore a little on the small side. This can sometimes leave me at a bit of a loss for something to say, so on more than one occasion I have ended up trying to teach an audience of Americans Cockney rhyming-slang instead. Call it my revenge for Dick Van Dyke's 'authentic' performance as a chimney-sweep in *Mary Poppins*.

Not all conventions happen on dry land. One of the things I have enjoyed most in the last few years is cruising, especially when it involves travelling to exotic places in gloriously sunny weather.

Not all of them do. I recall one or two less than idyllic cruises across the North Sea or English Channel, where a punishing schedule of on-board signing has been followed by a lengthy coach-trip to some fairly desolate and nondescript destination, there to sign photos, provided by the management, of course, and autographs for quite a long time, sustained only by the odd glass of Coke or Pepsi, before getting back on the coach, then back on the boat, docking just in time to catch a slow train to London, there to arrive exhausted, feeling slightly sick and not much richer for the experience.

On the other hand ... One of the best cruises I have been on was out of Miami, Florida, sailing around the Caribbean. Frazer Hines and I travelled out to Miami together, but as we were both in self-indulgent mode we used the excuse of the flight to Miami being far too long to endure in coach, aka standard, or cattle-class; you know, the bit of the aircraft where the seats are too close together, there's next-to-no legroom for people more than three-foot-six in height and you're always made to sit next to somebody who's too young, too large, too noisy or all of the above so your chances of getting any sleep are pretty slim.

We decided to treat ourselves to a better class of flight. Mentioning no names, it's suffice to say that luxury was uppermost in our minds when we decided which class to choose. How the other half live! Not for us the dreary hauling of luggage trollies across a crowded concourse in the hope of reaching our gate before it closed, nor even the joy of paying too much for mediocre coffee in a seating area occupied for the most part (and using about four chairs per person) by students or gap-year travellers with tatty rucksacks and untidy hairstyles.

We arrived at the terminal in a friend's car. We had already told the airline about that car so the barrier opened automatically on our approach; we drove up a long ramp to a large covered area where smiling and cheerful people relived us of our luggage, which we wouldn't see again until we reached Miami, and ushered us towards free champagne and other delights. We drank a fair amount of bubbly before heading off in different directions, Frazer for a complimentary manicure, I for a shoulder-and-neck massage. After that we enjoyed a couple of games of pool – free, I think; I don't remember having to put any money in the machines – and a bit more champagne. It was wonderful.

We enjoyed it so much that I think we would have opted out of flying and stayed there if we could. As that wasn't really a possibility, we just had a bit more fizz before heading for the aircraft which, after a very short walk we boarded.

We were immediately conducted to our pre-assigned seats (which, of course, converted into full-length beds when it was time to sleep) and served with yet more champagne. I dread to think how many French vineyards would be forced to close if the airline concerned ever went out of business. All that free champagne had put us in the mood for yet more drinks, so once we were safely airborne we went to the bar where we stayed until it was time for lunch. I can only commend the airline concerned for its caring attitude and understanding of the needs of Thespians in transit.

In due course, and after several Grey Goose vodka-and-tonics, we returned to our seats, just in time for lunch. And what a lunch it was! First rate food and really good wine, all served on proper plates with real cutlery and highly polished glasses. Down in the cheap seats they were probably eating motorway-service area style food served in disposable dishes with plastic cutlery, the latter being, of course, a counter-terrorism measure. Evidently bombers, hijackers and the like are too poor to travel in the posh part of the plane. Either that or the security services are especially diligent when it comes to vetting the better-off prospective passengers. All joking apart, though, the cabin staff couldn't have been friendlier or more helpful, not to mention generous. As we were leaving the aircraft they presented us each with a bottle of champagne and told us what a joy it had been to serve us. Apparently we were their favourite passengers ever!

All in all, this was a wonderful start to what turned out to be more of a holiday than a convention. We didn't have to sell photos and most of the fans on board already had our autographs so all we had to do was mingle with the *Who* fans, a small but significant minority of the ship's several thousand passengers, and generally have fun.

Leaving Miami, the ship took us all around the Caribbean and also to the coast of South America. I hope you won't be too jealous when I tell you that we went to Jamaica, Grand Cayman, Cozumel, Aruba, the Dominican Republic , Roatán and Belize. If you want to turn a really deep shade of green just look up some of these places up; they are all very beautiful and well worth visiting.

Frazer and I both wished we could have spent more time in most of them, but we deny visiting our money in Grand Cayman. As if all that weren't enough though, we didn't come straight home after the cruise. Instead we were invited to spend five days at Disneyland, Florida. What a place! Perhaps it's because actors never really grow up. Maybe we are all Peter Pan at heart. The Dr Who Sci-Fi Cruise is an ongoing yearly event so we get to visit the glorious Caribbean on a regular basis.

A man called George Fuller Golden, himself a founder of the White Rats, a trade union for American Vaudeville performers, while writing about the Grand Order of Water Rats, described actors as 'All geniuses of laughter and song; all boys – just boys'. Golden was an admirer of the Water Rats and Frazer and I are both proud members (I will say more about the Water Rats later on).

Perhaps the Disney people have come to appreciate that no matter how great they make their resort for kids they probably won't get repeat business if they don't hook the accompanying adults as well.

Whilst conventions in the UK are for the most part really enjoyable I have to confess that the ones in America are usually better in terms of the fun the celebrity guests can have, mostly because whereas most of the UK ones involve one night away from home in a decent hotel near the venue, the Stateside ones involve a lot more travelling (obviously) and more nights away, with days left free for sightseeing.

I went to a convention in Clarksville, Tennessee, though not on the last train and I *did* make it home. 'Last Train to Clarksville' was an anti-war song by manufactured 60s pop-group, The Monkees, said to be about a young man drafted for military service on his way to a training camp in Clarksville. Aware that he would probably serve in Viet Nam he expressed doubts about his chances of survival in the last line of the song, 'And I don't know if I'm ever coming home.' From Clarksville we were taken on to Nashville, a town where you can barely escape the sound of rock music as it pours out of every café and bar. Fortunately, I like that sort of music and if you ever travel in my car you'll probably be forced to listen to the legendary King of Rock and Roll, Elvis Presley, who recorded many hits at the famous RCA studios in Nashville. Several of us were lucky enough to get a guided tour of those studios. We were given a short talk before being shown the studio he actually recorded in. I was even allowed to sit at the piano Presley played.

CHAPTER TWELVE

HEARING VOICES

I promised you a little more about a couple of things: voice-overs and the Grand Order of Water Rats. No, the two aren't really connected other than by the fact that I made promises to you and I'm sure you've been waiting with bated breath for more on those subjects. I can't blame you – it's exciting stuff.

So, to voice-overs; even today, and despite a certain reluctance to spend the sums dished out in years gone by, these remain one of the best sources of funds available to the acting profession; short of becoming a hit-man for the mob, how else can you come by thousands of pounds for just a few minutes' work?

I was lucky a few years ago to have the sort of voice that big companies thought would appeal to potential customers. Back in those days actors were paid for each use of their voice on air; I suspect the bean-counters were a bit slow to appreciate how that would mount up if they advertised on TV. I'm sure you've noticed how often you see (and hear!) the same commercial over and over again, ad nauseam. Apparently, and surprisingly, nausea is not something that puts people off buying things. You may hate a commercial to the point that you want to run screaming from the room whenever it comes on, but it still does its job of making you want to buy things.

Thus it was that I made large amounts of money from saying …

but NO! I nearly mentioned the product there but I'm not being paid by them any more so I won't! Suffice to say that simply for praising a certain brand of instant coffee for its properties of richness and smoothness in two separate commercials I was paid a lot of money. The company concerned was so pleased with the results that it paid me yet more for allowing its advertising department to keep using those two four-second recordings for some two or three years.

Similar things happened with a certain brand of luxury car and with products designed to extend the working life of certain domestic white-goods. You may recall the memorable phrases I was paid to employ, so in the interests of fairness to those firms' competitors I should at this juncture point out that other instant coffees, cars and de-scaling agents are available.

If you do remember those voice-overs it may well be because you recognised my voice at the time; it was on heard quite often in TV and radio dramas. The advertisers might therefore arguably have been getting 'celebrity endorsement' if not on the cheap then at a very reasonable price, certainly a lot less than they would have to pay, say, Gary Lineker, Michael Parkinson or Philip Schofield. I wonder how many used cars the last-named has disposed of lately? Does Parky have over-fifty's life insurance? And if he's that keen on snacking on fried potato products how does Mr Lineker stay so slim?

The downside of all that, though, is that if your voice gets to be well known in association with one product, or even a range of different products, it can't be used by the manufacturer's competitors, and you become the victim of your own success. Factor in changing fashions and tastes and a voice-over artist's shelf-life becomes a bit limited. I live in the hope that my voice will be back in vogue again soon.

You might be wondering what all the fuss is about. Any fool can sit in front of a microphone and read a script. You don't have to be Johnny Mills or David Garrick to do that, do you? You might even think that because you can do a few silly voices to amuse your kids or your mates down the pub you have a natural talent, so you should be the one being paid thousands of pounds for a few seconds' work. Maybe you're right, but I have to tell you that you very probably aren't.

Voice acting is in many ways harder to do than visual acting. Apart from anything else you can't rely on facial expressions or body-language to help convey meaning. The microphone that can detect the raising of an eyebrow and the loudspeaker that can convey the result convincingly have yet to be invented. You have no alternative but to make your voice do all the work, and it's not always easy. Injecting an emotion into your voice so that people can judge your mood is far from easy; from deep melancholy to delirious happiness, from mild irritation through fury to downright murderousness and all feasible combinations to be judged just by listening not to what you say but to how you say it. If you're lucky and have a reasonably flexible voice with a good range of timbre, pitch and volume you are probably better placed than those who can only manage a rather dreary monotone. That said, lately some of the latter type seem to be getting the sort of voice-over work I would jump at. It's probably just as well you can't hear me saying that.

Then there are accents. Most people can do one or two different ones and keep them up reasonably convincingly for a couple of minutes, but how would they get on if they had to maintain them consistently over a period of weeks, months or even years? That takes talent and determination. If you've ever listened to Radio 4's *The Archers* (and I'm sure some of you will have done, though you might perhaps be reluctant to admit it) you will know that few of the main characters use their natural accents. You may remember a character called Mike Tucker, for example. That was not his normal voice. If you want to know what he really sounds like listen to the voice of Davros, the evil arch-Dalek, in *Doctor Who – Revelation of the Daleks*. It really is the same actor, Terry Molloy, but I should avoid possible legal action by stressing that I was joking about his real voice being like the ones that repeat 'Exterminate' over and over.

Audiences are sensitive to change, and will notice if a Birmingham accent suddenly reverts to RP or changes to Liverpudlian for an instant. RP, or Received Pronunciation, is regarded by many as the gold standard of speech. It was what my elocution teacher at Conti's strove to instil in me, and used to be compulsory for BBC announcers and newsreaders. However, even that has changed. Try comparing recordings of Her Majesty at the time of her accession to more modern ones; you don't have to be a Henry Higgins to spot how even the Queen's English seems to have evolved. Many regular listeners find changes in accent unsettling, which may be why characters tend to get written out rather than simply re-cast when an actor becomes unavailable.

'Fine,' you say, 'but for just those few seconds of a commercial it surely can't matter that much?' Sorry; wrong again. TV air-time is an expensive commodity, and advertising agencies know their clients are reluctant to see (or hear!) it wasted. Voice-over artists don't just sit in front of a microphone reading a script. They sit in a booth and their performance is monitored throughout by a sound engineer who will stop them if they're going too fast or too slow, and will also pounce on any slight blemish – an unwitting clearing of the throat, or a muffled hiccough perhaps – and send them back to the beginning. You have to get the pitch, intonation and timing just right, and that can take a long time. You might have to work for as long as twenty minutes for your thousands of pounds, and then there's the time taken getting to the studios in the first place. They don't pay you for that!

If you spend any time at all working in the entertainment profession you will probably encounter the Grand Order of Water Rats. I first heard about them when I started at Conti's, and a lot of the people I've worked with have been members. So what is it?

Well, a long time ago in the north-east of England, the sport of trotting was quite popular. I believe these days it's more common in the USA. You will rarely see it on British TV. Basically, two or more horses each pull a light-weight cart with a driver on board over a pre-determined course, and the first one to cross the finish line wins. Back in 1889 there was one particular pony that was always worth backing. His name at that time was the Magpie so it shouldn't be too difficult to guess what colour he was. The secret apparently lay in the way he was trained. At times when there was nobody around the Magpie's owner would take him to the start-line and let him have a quick munch from his nosebag – one mouthful, no more! He was then driven a mile down the road, turned round and driven back to the start/finish line, where he was allowed to gorge himself on as much as he could eat. The Magpie pretty soon realised that the faster he covered the course, the sooner he got his oats. Come race-day over the same course, he had a far greater incentive than his rivals to complete the race, and the owner, having presumably made a fair number of bets, was more than able to afford to reward the Magpie with another well-filled nosebag.

It wasn't long, though, until the good betting-folk of South Shields cottoned on to the Magpie's winning ways and developed a reluctance to offer decent odds on the animal. His owner, Mr Richard Thornton, was quite a wealthy individual even without the Magpie's winnings, and had at the time control of a chain of variety theatres. A certain Professor James Finney (as he was styled on theatre posters of the time) and his sister Marie were headlining at one of those theatres, performing various daring feats in a large glass water tank. The Professor became friendly with Mr Thornton and on one occasion accompanied him to the race track where he saw the Magpie run. It occurred to one or both of those gentlemen that moving the horse to London might prove lucrative. Even in those days there was more money to be found in London, as well as a whole host of potential punters who knew nothing of the animal's prowess.

Accordingly, a syndicate was formed, the horse transported to London and a racing buggy purchased. The horse was re-trained (using the well-proven oat-feast method) over a one-mile course, now believed to have run between Thornton Heath and a public house in Streatham, South London. The Magpie soon became very popular, and turned out on most Sunday mornings, regardless of the weather. One day after a race he was being driven home, still attached to his buggy. The weather was appalling. If Noah had been around he'd have been reaching for his toolbox. The poor horse was drenched. The driver of a passing horse-drawn omnibus saw him and inquired, perhaps with a hint of mockery, as to the nature of the beast. On being told that the Magpie was a 'trotter' he replied, 'Blimey! It looks more like a bleedin' water rat!' The name must have appealed to the Professor, and it was readily approved by the rest of the syndicate; the Magpie raced under his new name thereafter.

After one particularly successful Sunday morning's racing a group of about ten music-hall artistes decided to celebrate their success. They travelled by coach-and-four from the Canterbury public house in Westminster Bridge Road out to a pub called The Magpie in Sunbury where they dined exceedingly well, so well in fact that they decided to form a sort of club with the aim of enjoying similar social events in the future, and in honour of the animal whose speed and endurance in that morning's race had enabled them to celebrate in lavish style they decided to call themselves Pals of the Water Rat.

From such humble beginnings, a rumbustious group of variety artistes on a spree, arose the Grand Order of Water Rats, a much respected charitable institution which boasts royalty amongst its associate membership. Only professional performers can be full members, and so far no heirs to the throne have taken up a second career as acrobat or stand-up comedian. Maybe one day?

It has to be said that the main aim of the Rats is to enjoy themselves, in keeping with the goal of the original Pals on that night in Sunbury, but of almost the same importance is the charitable work of the Order. Many people and organisations have benefitted from the Order's generosity, not least the Evelina London Children's Hospital where my greatly loved and missed grandson Oliver was treated so well for a long time. The Rats recently funded a well-equipped music room, open for use by all patients at the hospital. The allocation of funds for such causes is part of the serious business conducted at meetings of the Order, that's when it can be fitted in between the sort of hilarity you would expect when the critical mass of comedians is exceeded.

I never really expected to be able to join such an august and prestigious organisation, and probably wouldn't have been able to had I been a better golfer, for I would then probably have joined a real golf-club rather than the Vaudeville Golfing Society (VGS) that I joined a few years ago. There was, and still is, considerable overlap between that organisation, whose aim is to provide affordable golf-related activities for entertainment professionals, and the Water Rats.

It was through the VGS that I became friendly with Kaplan Kaye, who like his father, the comedian and actor Davy Kaye, is a past King Rat, though I'm assured that title is not hereditary. Kaplan is a well-known actor and musician and currently one half of a very talented and entertaining musical duo, the *Ukaye Ukes* who as their name suggests do amazing things with ukuleles, singing and playing to backing tracks featuring other instruments, but all played by them. The other member, fellow Rat Bill Dare, is also a talented musician, having worked with the Rolling Stones, the Strawbs, Paul McCartney and many others. They tell me they are available for dances, Masonics, bar mitzvahs etc. (OK, boys – I promised you a plug; now about that pint …)

To cut what is already perhaps too long a story a little bit short, I was playing golf at a VGS event and I asked Kaplan how I should go about joining the Rats. He said I should start by getting myself proposed and seconded and then with my proposer and seconder attend a few evenings at the Water Rats' pub in Kings Cross where I would be able to get to know and more importantly, get known by some of the Rats, although I wouldn't be allowed to go into their lodge-room. If after that I still felt I'd like to join, my name could be put forward, and in due course a ballot would be held and I'd be told if I were in or out.

My original proposer was the disc-jockey Ed 'Stewpot' Stewart, and my friend Frazer Hines agreed to second me. All seemed to be going to plan, until Ed's untimely death in January 2016, when the process ground to a halt. Frazer then agreed that he would propose me; all I had to do was to find a seconder. Fortunately by then I had been to a few meetings (despite the hardship of having to sit downstairs in the bar while the Rats held their Lodge meeting) and one of the people I had met, a comedian called Jeff Stevenson, agreed to step into the breach. I was then kept on tenterhooks for a few months until finally being told that I had been accepted for initiation.

I was delighted when the news came through, though also more than a little nervous. However, on 4th September 2016 I was indeed initiated into the Rats. My number is 899. There can only be 200 Water Rats at any given time; it's a bit 'dead men's shoes', but what shoes to fill! Those currently attempting that feat include the Hairy Bikers, Alfie Boe and Jimmy Osmond.

As soon as my own ceremony was over I phoned my wife, Sally, who seemed to be quite proud of me, so much so that she straight away rang our daughter, Lucy, and said, 'Your Dad's a Rat!'

Lucy's initial reaction: 'Why? What's he done now?'

Oh, the joys of parenthood …

The time has come for me to bring the curtain down on these ramblings. My career in Show Business began sixty-four years ago. It has been both joyful and rewarding. I have met and dined with royalty, worked with many 'big names' in film, played leading roles in numerous television productions and appeared in theatres up and down the country, from the North of Scotland to the South of England and almost everywhere in between. The West End's theatres beckoned; I answered the call and enjoyed considerable success.

So what does the future hold for me now? I do believe I can hear my phone ringing … so, dear reader, with your permission I will answer it and hopefully find out.

ABOUT THE AUTHOR

Colin Spaull is a British actor who has worked in theatre, television and film and who is especially noted for his television work being one of only a handful of actors to appear in both the original and the new series of *Doctor Who*. He has become a familiar face, and voice, to British television audiences.

Colin's lead roles have included Ronnie Winslow in *The Winslow Boy*, Venables in *Jennings goes to School*, Pip in *Great Expectations* and Dickon Sowerby in *The Secret Garden*. Over the years he has been a regular in popular soaps, dramas, sitcoms, sci-fi adventures and sketch shows.

In Colin's view a third appearance in *Doctor Who* would usefully round off his long and varied career.

TELEVISION APPEARANCES
Dixon of Dock Green

All My Sons

Jennings At School

Great Expectations

Ask For King Billy

Get Back

The Secret Garden

A Brother For Joe

Heidi

Stranger On The Shore

The Benny Hill Show

Detective

Theatre 625

Z Cars

Blackmail

No Hiding Place

Thirty Minute Theatre

The Fellows

The Wednesday Play

The Gnomes Of Dulwich

Sykes and a Referee

Sykes and a Holiday

She: The Seven Faces Of Woman

The Brontes Of Howarth

Agony

L For Lester

The Bill

Dr Who

Boon

Birds Of A Feather

The House Of Elliot

Minder

Little Beggars

The Brittas Empire

Goodnight Sweetheart

Nelsons Column

The Detectives
Morse
'Orrible
Down To Earth
Judge John Deed
The Murder Game
Holby City
Casualty
Doctors
The Last Detective
The Courtroom
Citizen James
Yorky
Television Club
The Frankie Howard Show
Barney Is My Darling
The Sullivan Brothers
The Larkins
Crossroads
Coronation Street
Eastenders
Conceptions Of Murder
Watch This Space
The Collectors
The Bretts
Streets Apart
London's Burning
Shine On Harvey Moon

Maisie Raine

The Inbetweeners

The Hour

The Catherine Tate Show

Present Laughter

Drama 67

The Bed Sit Girl

THEATRE PRODUCTIONS

The Remarkable Mr Pennypacker

The Happiest Days Of Your Life

The Winslow Boy

Present Laughter

Richard The Third

Titus Andronicus

Spring Awakening

The Fourth Of June

The Tempest

Outside Edge

Ten Times Table

Henry VI

Arsenic and Old Lace

Little Malcolm

Who Saw Him Die

How The Other Half Loves

Never So Good

FILMS

Before Winter Comes

Heavens Above

Frenzy

Make Aliens Dance

Eat Yourself Slim

Redemption Road

AUDIO PRODUCTIONS

Big Finish

Dr Zhivago BBC radio play

Numerous narrations and voice-overs

If you have enjoyed this book, please leave a review for Colin to let him know what you thought of his work.

You can find out more about Colin on his author page on the Fantastic Books Store. While you're there, why not browse our delightful tales and wonderfully woven prose?

www.fantasticbooksstore.com

Printed in Great Britain
by Amazon